D1106431

PERSPECTIVES
ON PORNOGRAPHY

WITHDRAWN

PERSPECTIVES
ON PORNOGRAPHY

EDITED WITH AN INTRODUCTION BY
Douglas A. Hughes

ST. MARTIN'S PRESS
NEW YORK

AFFILIATED PUBLISHERS: Macmillan & Company, Limited,
London—also at Bombay, Calcutta, Madras and Melbourne—
The Macmillan Company of Canada, Limited, Toronto.

ACKNOWLEDGMENTS & COPYRIGHT NOTICES

Alberto Moravia, "Eroticism in Literature." Reprinted with the permission Farrar, Straus & Giroux, Inc. from *Man as an End* by Alberto Moravia. Copyright © 1965 by Martin Secker & Warburg Ltd.

Anthony Burgess, "What Is Pornography?" Reprinted from *Urgent Copy* by Anthony Burgess, by permission of W. W. Norton & Company, Inc. and Jonathan Cape Ltd. Copyright © 1968 by Anthony Burgess.

Harry Levin, "The Unbanning of the Books." Reprinted by permission of the author. Copyright © 1966 by Harry Levin. First published in *Atlantic Monthly*.

Stanley Edgar Hyman, "In Defense of Pornography." Reprinted by permission of the publisher, Horizon Press, from *Standards: A Chronicle of Books for Our Time* by Stanley Edgar Hyman. Copyright 1966.

Paul Goodman, "Pornography, Art, and Censorship." Copyright © 1961 by Paul Goodman. Source: *Commentary*. Another version of this essay appears in *Utopian Essays and Practical Proposals*, by Paul Goodman. Reprinted by permission of Random House, Inc.

Peter Michelson, "An Apology for Pornography." Reprinted by permission of *The New Republic*, © 1966, Harrison-Blaine of New Jersey, Inc.

George P. Elliott, "Against Pornography." Reprinted by permission of Georges Borchardt, Inc. Copyright © 1965 by *Harper's Magazine*, Inc.

George Steiner, "Night Words: High Pornography and Human Privacy." From *Language and Silence* by George Steiner. Copyright © 1965, 1967 by George Steiner. Reprinted by permission of Atheneum Publishers and Faber & Faber, Ltd.

Kenneth Tynan, "Dirty Books Can Stay." Reprinted by permission of Curtis Brown, Ltd. Copyright © 1968 by Kenneth Tynan. First published in *Esquire Magazine*.

Ernest van den Haag, "The Case for Pornography Is the Case for Censorship and Vice Versa." Reprinted by permission of the author. Copyright © 1967 by Ernest van den Haag. First published in *Esquire Magazine*; slightly revised for this volume.

Susan Sontag, "The Pornographic Imagination." Reprinted with the permission of Farrar, Straus & Giroux, Inc. from *Styles of Radical Will* by Susan Sontag. Copyright © 1966 by Susan Sontag.

For Richard Shereikis

CONTENTS

Introduction

"AS OUR VITALITY EBBS," MALCOLM MUGGERIDGE HAS WRITTEN, "people reach out for vicarious excitement, like the current sex mania in pop songs and the popular press. At the decline and fall of the Roman Empire, the works of Sappho, Catullus, and Ovid were celebrated. There is an analogy in that for us." Some Americans, alarmed by the apparently unrestrained hedonism of the young and calculated obscenity of today's writers and actors, would be quick to apply this wry analogy to contemporary America. This small but vocal minority really believes that the cultural permissiveness of the last decade, with its refreshing openness, candor, and sincerity, is plunging the nation into moral decay and ultimate ruin. In the view of our moral guardians (perhaps better regarded as mores managers) the artistic expressions of eroticism which have arisen in the last few years are proof that a spiritual dry rot is undermining society. We are morally sick and are perverting our young, they say, and they point to the rise of obscenity and public nudity, to *Portnoy's Complaint* and *Oh! Calcutta!* Recently Billy Graham, his eyes fixed on New York City, asserted that certain areas of the country "have sunk as low as anything in history." And then inevitably the poor, effete Romans, who always seem to be waiting in the wings in any discussion of decadence, are once again called in as an instructive analogy for Americans of the relationship of immoderate erotic interests and social decadence.

Without conceding the imminent fall of the American Empire, one may grant that Americans, particularly the young, are indeed reaching out as never before for vicarious and real erotic excitements which are supplied, in part, by contemporary Ovids and Sapphos. There is no gainsaying the new and unashamed emphasis placed on the senses and sexuality in what may be called post-Puritan America. As any adult is aware, we are indeed living through a sexual revolution, and this overturning of the old constricted, parochial attitude toward sex is another example of the honesty we have come to associate with what is best in contemporary society. Far from being a signal of moral decline or the ebbing of our vitality, the acceptance of the senses and the thoroughgoing liberalization of sexual attitudes are, I believe, signs of vigor and health. They are indications that America may at long last be divesting itself of the crippling immature notions of sexuality and the functions of the human body which have characterized this nation since the arrival of the Puritans. No doubt without deliberately intending to, the participants in the sexual revolution are obviously preparing the ground for new sexual standards and are leading the whole country willy-nilly to another and more mature level of eroticism.

One of the predictable, and for some distressing, developments of this new attitude toward sex has been the publication and widespread distribution of erotically stimulating literature—pornography—an example of Mr. Muggeridge's "vicarious excitement." Pornography has suddenly become a bulky and lucrative element in novels, films, and dramas, and it has become, as suburban mothers and others are wont to complain, as handy as the local supermarket or drugstore. The present uneasy tolerance of pornography in the United States is really a remarkable phenomenon, a situation so revolutionary that it would have been regarded as virtually impossible ten years ago. As recently as 1960 a colleague of mine grappled with the U.S. Customs Bureau in an effort to import Henry Miller's novels from France for a critical study. Not only are Miller's works now published here and available in the bookstores of even religious universities, but recent rulings by the Supreme Court on questions of obscenity have had the effect of allowing the publication and sale of virtually any book. In fact, Americans can now openly purchase books that are banned in France, such as *Story of O*. Aware of rapidly changing mores and faced with open-minded judgments by literary critics, the courts as well as most politicians have acquiesced, at least for the moment, to the high level of sexual titillation in artistic and not-so-artistic works. As Anthony Lewis observed a few years ago in *Esquire*, "Today the voice of the sophisticated critic is dominant, and the Philistines are on the run."

Not all literary critics, however, speak with the same sophisticated voice on the question of pornography, as this collection of essays testifies. The fourteen distinguished novelists and critics in this symposium vigorously disagree on the nature, value, and social implications of erotically arousing writing. On the one hand are a few who regard pornography as an unmitigated good and the right of each person, while on the other are some who argue for its suppression:

most of the contributors stand between these two extreme points of view. Each responds in his own way to one or both of what I take to be the two fundamental questions surrounding pornography: what are the psychological *effects* of pornographic works on the normal individual, as manifested in moral and social behavior; and to what extent may pornography be judged as legitimate literature rather than merely ersatz eroticism.*

To believe that pornographic works have no psychological effects is as absurd as asserting that readers of fiction are not influenced in some way by what they experience imaginatively. But contrary to the dogmatic pronouncements of Billy Graham and the well-known PTA sermonizers, no scientific evidence is yet available to indicate clearly the kind and degree of pornography's influence on the individual. Is pornography a corrupting force and does it subvert human values? Does it stimulate aggressive sexual impulses and thus lead to unnecessary, avertable sex crimes? Does it encourage voyeurism, fetishism, and masturbatory fantasies, warping the person's view of sexuality and love? Or does pornography serve a useful, almost therapeutic purpose for some persons, relaxing rather than stimulating sexual impulses?

Although these questions cannot be answered unequivocally, at least for the moment, with scientific facts, there is cogent information from Denmark, information which has become available since most of the essays in this book were written, that suggests that pornography is decidedly not a corrupter of the mind or a moral threat to society. In 1967 Denmark became the first Western country to legalize all forms of pornography, including the hardest of the hard-core variety, in an experiment which may eventually affect the legal and governmental thinking on pornography in other countries. To be sure, all the facts are not yet in, but the ini-

---

* The main focus of this book is on pornographic writing as opposed to the photographic and cinematic varieties, and most of the contributors are not directly concerned with censorship and the law as they relate to pornography.

tial findings are encouraging. For example, although crime in general is rising in Denmark as it is everywhere else, sex crimes have declined measurably since restrictions on pornography were abolished; sex crimes in Copenhagen dropped 34 per cent between the end of 1966 and the end of 1967 and have remained at a lower level up to the present. Such figures tend to undermine the moral case against pornography. Some Danish psychologists are more convinced than ever that such vicarious erotic excitements are far from being pernicious for some people, and the Danish Medical-Legal Council, in a report supporting the legalization of pornography, wrote: "Conversations with sexual neurotics will almost invariably reveal that in their childhood any mention of sexual subjects was tabooed in their homes. One gets the impression that they have been told too little about sex life and that they have read too little rather than too much erotic literature." The Council's report observed that the sexual attitudes of youngsters are almost wholly determined by parents and peers, and concluded, "It is inconceivable that coarse external influences such as pornography should be of any significance in the sexual development of children and adolescents." Not surprisingly, legalization is also having the effect of improving the quality of erotic offerings, because it seems that once pornography is freely available and people are allowed to satisfy their curiosity, they tend to tire quickly of the crass, one-dimensional variety.

The question whether pornography may be regarded as literature is debatable on purely aesthetic grounds, and the members of the symposium in this book address themselves to this point with considerable ingenuity. Perhaps this question may be simplified by separating works that are exclusively pornographic from those that utilize sexually exciting material as an adjunct to the narrative. In fact, some of us consider works pornographic that are only occasionally explicit in sexual descriptions or infrequently seek to arouse our erotic impulses. Nevertheless, pornography as respectable literature presents problems. Because pornography, by its very definition, is essentially concerned with arousing the reader sexually, it is obvious that its effects are going to be severely limited regardless of the skill and subtlety of the writer. However artistic the pornographer may be, he will succeed in evoking only one narrow response, something we do not commonly associate with literature. Even those works only peripherally pornographic often swing dangerously close to the shoals of the unconscious and its repressed materials and thus may provoke discomforting anxieties even when the writer maintains rigorous formal structures (form in literature being a means of *mitigating* anxiety). Richard Gilman, the former literary editor of *The New Republic,* offers a distinction between pornography and imaginative writing which focuses on sexual themes, writing that it is "useful to retain 'pornography' as a term (without moral condemnation) to denote sexual writing that fails as literature." Quite plainly some essayists in this book would disagree with that statement.

The symposium entitled *Perspectives on Pornography* is opened, appropriately enough, by two well-known and respected contemporary novelists, Alberto Moravia and Anthony Burgess. Moravia, in a kind of foreword to the remarks of the other essayists, succinctly explains how eroticism in modern literature differs from the depiction of love in earlier periods. To those who object to the explicit dramatization of sex in the fiction of our time, Moravia replies, "in the modern world sex is synonymous with love, and who could deny that love is a very common subject in the literature of all times and places?" In "What Is Pornography?" Burgess seeks to distinguish pornography from literary art. He considers pornography "harmless so long as we do not corrupt our taste by mistaking it for literature." Noting that a pornographic work is an instrument for achieving sexual catharsis, Burgess, echoing the remarks of Joyce's Stephen Dedalus, points out that didactic and pornographic works expect the discharge of stimulation in reality, whereas the "purpose of literary art is to arouse emotions and discharge those emotions as part of the artistic experience."

Harry Levin's contribution, "The Unbanning of the Books," is an interesting historical review of the efforts to suppress great and not-so-great novels since the 1920's. Professor Levin, who is chairman of Harvard's comparative literature department, reminds us that many great novelists appeared initially in the midst of a *succès de scandale*. Beginning with discussions of *Ulysses* and *Lady Chatterley's Lover*, he recounts how attempts at banning erotic and partially pornographic fictions have failed throughout the years. With respect to the present situation, he believes that the new artistic freedoms may eventually drive pornography out of business; and if, he thinks, we can discard the judgment of whether a book is dirty or clean, "if we abandon censorship, we [will] depend all the more imperatively upon criticism."

With an engaging informality, Vivian Mercier touches on a number of interesting ideas concerning pornography's relation to man's sexual life and its relation to art. Unlike the other contributors, he expresses himself in a personal manner, beginning with the recounting of his own first experience with pornography as a boy in Ireland, and he is more observer than polemicist. A professor of English and a perceptive critic of modern French literature, Mercier is at his best in discussing the connection between eroticism and art. Writing on what he calls the "New Erotics," he suggests that artists have so far failed to utilize the new cultural freedoms to enlarge our understanding of sexuality. "The New Erotics," he writes, "would be a blend of art and science, written and illustrated by artists of one sex for the enlightenment of the other; its ultimate effect, I think, would be not only to help the sexes understand each other better but to bring their modes of sexual self-expression closer together."

The discussion moves on with a strong defense of pornography by Stanley Edgar Hyman, Paul Goodman, and Peter Michelson. Questioning the theory that pornography en-

courages sexual crimes or homosexuality, Hyman speaks can-
didly on its behalf. Pornographic "books may teach and encourage a wider range of heterosexual activity, oral and anal
as well as genital, and should be welcomed if they do." Paul
Goodman argues that censorship itself may be a cause of
perverse literature by inflating the desire for pornography,
and he points out what the Danish experiment has apparently shown, namely that legalized pornography would deplete the criminal market, an argument disputed further on
by Ernest van den Haag. Goodman's essay also treats the nature of pornography in relation to speech and art. Acknowledging the dearth of sensitive or even sophisticated pornography, he says, "The question is not *whether* pornography,
but the quality of the pornography." Peter Michelson follows with an *apologia* for pornography, anticipating the long
philosophical statement offered later in the discussion by
Susan Sontag. Like other defenders of erotic fiction, Michelson denies that pornography is a moral threat to the average
mind, adding that excessive interest in it may suggest an ab-
normality. "A preoccupation with pornography or any other
kind of romance may be an index of mental imbalance or
even potential criminality, but it is certainly not a cause."
Pornography, he argues, points to man's almost neurotic and
archetypal interest in sexuality; it is "for better or worse . . .
the imaginative record of man's sexual will." He raises other
noteworthy points, including the idea that pornography is
part of modern art's aesthetic of the ugly.

In fairness to the other side, two articulate opponents of
pornography are called on next to present their views.
George P. Elliott and George Steiner are both opposed to
pornography on the grounds that it is psychologically intrusive, offends the individual's privacy, and debases human
sexuality. Elliott begins by stating that he is against censorship as well as pornography. He would outlaw pornography
but would tolerate its existence as long as its readers did not
annoy their neighbors. This far-ranging essay plunges into
aesthetics and the alleged nihilism of pornographic writers,

and it controverts Paul Goodman's earlier remarks. George
Steiner's objections to pornography center on its putative violation of the human spirit. Pornographic works, he con-
tends, "leave a man less free, less himself, than they found
him; they leave language poorer. . . ." This sensitive literary
critic complains that erotic writing is invariably dull, that
pornographers do our imagining for us, leading us fatuously
through intimate sexual acts.

Kenneth Tynan, the drama critic and organizer of *Oh!
Calcutta!*, replies to Steiner: "*They do our imagining for us.
It sounds like a fearful affront, a chilling premonition of
1984; but in fact it is exactly what all good writers have done
since the birth of literature.*" Each man has the inalienable
right of *self*-abuse, argues Tynan, though not the right of
abusing others. Much of what he says appears to be corrobor-
ated by the already mentioned Danish experiment with pornography. Tynan maintains that pornographic works are a
boon to the lonely, the sexually confused, and the hopelessly
ugly who may employ them in masturbatory fantasies.

The next voice heard is that of social philosopher Ernest
van den Haag, who believes that pronography must be restricted or American society will become more anxious, brutal, de-individualized, and hedonistic than it already is. A
clear expression of the conservative perspective, his essay is
an attempt to outline a practical means by which literature
may be screened for the prurient depiction of sex. Pornography, he argues, should be controlled because it is an infantile fantasy without any foundation in reality, a sordid
dream in which sex is severed from its human context.

Susan Sontag's long essay, "The Pornographic Imagination," is perhaps the most impressive and meaningful expression in the symposium. Considering pornography as a literary genre that is occasionally significant though usually not,
Miss Sontag clearly explains why she disagrees with those
who deny that it can be serious literature. Interested in the
possibility that some pornographic works—represented by
Story of O and *The Story of the Eye*—may reach the level of

literary art, she refuses to grant importance to the psychological and social objections to pornography, a position fairly common among strictly literary critics. Miss Sontag's contribution to the symposium is a complex, in-depth examination of erotically stimulating literature in general with the analysis of some specific recent works. Along with Tynan and Goodman, she openly defends an author's right to arouse his reader sexually; a point difficult to contradict.

In "Pornography: A Trip Around the Halfworld" Felix Pollak, the curator of rare books at the University of Wisconsin Library, discusses pornography humorously and critically from several previously unvoiced points of view. His is a delightfully discursive, entertaining essay, ranging from the paradoxical need of censorship for good, imaginative pornography to a mild attack on erotically stimulating advertising which even contemporary Puritans accept, to a discussion of the threat of erotic art to society's unquestioned values and assumptions. Arguing that erotic art is deeply personal, Mr. Pollak writes, "The totalitarian and authoritarian countries take the threat [of pornography] seriously because hedonism in all its forms is a humanistic, liberalistic, and individualistic philosophy. . . ."

Like Moravia earlier, William Phillips focuses his remarks on the type or quality of sex in modern literature. The editor of *Partisan Review* argues persuasively that it is not a matter of just more sex in contemporary literature. There is in fact a new *kind* of sexuality, the very texture of literary sex is different from that of the past, and Mr. Phillips examines this sexual style in some detail. In the course of his article he comments on the earlier remarks in the symposium by Elliott, Steiner, and Miss Sontag.

It is clear by reading the newspaper, especially the local sheets, that despite the country's mild new erotic climate, pornographic literature is still feared, abhorred, and condemned by many people. Like the whore, it seems to be a pariah. Although the prejudice and misunderstanding surrounding the question of pornography will not be eradicated by the discussions presented here, most readers will find the essays—even those with which they disagree—informative as well as engaging. A few of them are nothing short of brilliant. As I have indicated, this book includes various points of view on pornography and, despite my own ideas, no attempt has been made to approve of or condemn such literature. I have sought to include pieces that are not only interesting and well written, but ones which are representative, essays expressing a singular perspective.

D.A.H.

Pullman, Washington
January 1970

PERSPECTIVES
ON PORNOGRAPHY

Alberto Moravia

Eroticism in Literature

EROTICISM IN MODERN LITERATURE HAS NO RESEMBLANCE TO
eroticism in pagan literature nor to eroticism in the literatures that followed it, though if there are any resemblances
at all these are to the former rather than the latter. But
there is the difference that in pagan literature eroticism has
all the innocence, brutality and cohesion of a nature not yet
divided and turned against itself by the Christian sense of
sin, whereas eroticism in modern literature is bound to take
the Christian experience into account. In other words, eroticism in modern literature derives not from a situation of na-

ture, but from a process of liberation from pre-existent prohibitions and taboos. With the pagans, freedom was an unconscious, simple fact, whereas with the moderns it has been
reclaimed, rediscovered, rewon. In compensation eroticism
in modern literature has, or should have, the character proper to subjects that neither shock nor draw undue attention
to themselves—that are, in short, normal if we understand
normal to mean the transformation of the sexual act into
something scientifically known and poetically valid, and
therefore insignificant from the ethical point of view.

The result of this is, or should be, that for the first time
since the pagan literatures sex is becoming material for poetry without the need for recourse to the props of symbols or
the disguises of metaphor. Today, for the first time for many
centuries, the sexual act can be represented directly, explicitly, realistically and poetically in a literary work, whenever
the work itself makes this necessary. At this point someone
will ask: but *is* it necessary to talk about the sexual act and,
if so, when? My answer is that it is not always necessary to
talk about the sexual act, just as it is not always necessary to
talk about social questions or adventures in Africa, but that,
as the prohibitions and taboos that stood in its way no
longer exist today, to pass it over in silence when it *is* necessary is no longer, as it once was, a moral question but an in-
adequacy of expression. To take an example: the contemporary writer who does not speak of the sexual act when the
subject-matter of his book requires it, is behaving like the
citizen who refrains from talking about politics in a democratic régime because the dictatorship that preceded it forbade him to do so. Of course, let me repeat, it is not always
necessary to talk about the sexual act; but it is necessary to
talk about it when—to make a play on words—it is necessary.

Our objector now asks why on earth it seems so often necessary to talk about the sexual act in modern literature. To
this we answer very simply that in the modern world sex is
synonymous with love, and who could deny that love is a

very common subject in the literatures of all times and places?

But how in the world, someone else will say, has love been transformed into sex in modern literature; in other words how has it lost the indirect, metaphorical and idealised character that it had in the past, to end up as identified with the sexual act? There are many reasons for this identification, the principal one being, as we have already pointed out, the collapse of the prohibitions and taboos that only too frequently and artificially lay at the root of the false idealisations of eroticism.

These taboos and prohibitions were only in appearance of Christian origin; in reality Christianity confined itself to counselling chastity. Probably the taboos and prohibitions were the outcome of a slow social involution, an involution not unlike the one that can be observed in, for instance, class relationships in some Western societies.

However, the collapse of these taboos and prohibitions has been caused mainly by what is called depth psychology, or psychoanalysis and the related psychological sciences. The discoveries of psychoanalysis have had a crucial result in two ways: they have broken down the taboos, and have raised the sexual act from the ignominy into which the taboos had cast it, and have reinstated it among the few ways of expression and communion available to man.

The sexual act in modern literature is, or should be, neither diabolical temptation, as with the medieval ascetics, nor an almost gastronomical pleasure as with the eighteenth-century bourgeoisie, but as it shows itself when we manage to separate it both from moralistic horror and vulgar hedonism: an act of insertion into a cosmic and superhuman order. Seen in this way the sexual act is effectively something higher, more mysterious, and more complete than love, especially if love is interpreted as the simple physico-sentimental relationship between man and woman.

Anthony Burgess

What Is Pornography?

AFTER THE DEVALUATION ANNOUNCEMENT AND THOSE THREAT-
ening words about England being a proud country, after the
Daily Mirror's dollifying of thinned sterling as the "perky
mini-pound," I knew what the verdict on *Last Exit to
Brooklyn* would have to be: it was just one of those weeks. I
had hoped, even after the Marlborough Street magistrate's
wonder that post-Zola novelists were not satisfied with the
reticence of *Vanity Fair,* that sense would prevail in the
higher court, and that eminent men of letters would not be
dismissed as fools or smuthounds. But a man of God and for-

mer Test captain testified that *Last Exit* had injured him to an extent he could not yet assess (this presumably means *corrupted* him), and mere *littérateurs* knew the case was lost.

Despite David Sheppard's evidence, the question whether fiction can morally corrupt a normal mind still seems to me to be an open one. To say that a book can have no moral influence at all is probably nonsense, but the moral influence of works of literary art, as opposed to didactic works, must be regarded as very much in doubt. Arguments addressed to reason or to prejudice—*Il Principe, Das Kapital, Mein Kampf*—have radically determined the moral beliefs of whole nations, but there is little evidence that a book which merely represents life, however one-sidedly, can change the code of behavior of a healthy mind. We must remember, when using this term, that behavior is of social or legal import only when it concerns more than one person. The law, if not the Scout Code, permits onanism, solitary bondage, and self-flagellation.

A pornographic work represents social acts of sex, frequently of a perverse or wholly fantastic nature, often without consulting the limits of physical possibility. Such works encourage solitary fantasy, which is then usually quite harmlessly discharged in masturbation. A pornographic book is, then, an instrument for procuring a sexual catharsis, but it rarely promotes the desire to achieve this through a social mode, an act of erotic congress: the book is, in a sense, a substitute for a sexual partner. A pornograph can be either verbal or visual, but the visual stimulus is generally more intense than the verbal one. If anything that encourages sexual fantasy and leads to onanistic discharge is a pornograph, then pornographs lie all about us—underwear advertisements, the provocative photographs in the non-class Sunday papers. Etymologically (*porne* is Greek for "whore") any depersonalized picture of a possible sexual partner represents the purest pornography you can get; how much more stimulating, though, is a real girl in a miniskirt. Women cannot help moving, and men cannot help being moved.

A pornographic work and a didactic work (like Smiles's *Self-help*) have this in common: they stimulate, and expect the discharge of the stimulation to be effected in real-life acts—acts of masturbation or acts of social import. They differ from a work of literature in that the purpose of literary art is to arouse emotions and discharge those emotions as part of the artistic experience. This is what Aristotle meant by his implied doctrine of catharsis (the full explication of this has been left to his commentators). If we read a book or see a play or film and are then driven to discharge the aroused emotion in some solitary or social act, then we have experienced good pornography or good didacticism but very bad art. Where *Last Exit to Brooklyn* possibly fails as good art is in its arousing of our social conscience to the extent of our wanting to do something charitable to people whose tragic lives arouse Aristotelian pity and terror. The book is over-didactic, then. In that it does not conduce to a desire for sexual discharge it is not pornographic. Twelve good men have made an error of classification.

Pornography, as I have indicated, is harmless so long as we do not corrupt our taste by mistaking it for literature. But it has been alleged, most recently by Lady Snow in her book on the Moors Murders, that a pornographic work may induce unstable minds to carry over the fantasy element, particularly when it involves elements of cruelty, to real life. Brady apparently read the Marquis de Sade, and his crime was nauseatingly sadistic. It is, I think, all too likely that Sade helped to stimulate a nature already perverse, but a perverse nature can be stimulated by anything. Any book can be used as a pornographic instrument, even a great work of literature, if the mind that so uses it is off balance. I once found a small boy masturbating in the presence of the Victorian steel-engravings in a family Bible. Blood-drinking murderers have admitted to the stimulation of the sacrifice of the Mass. One multiple child-murderer in the United States was, on his own confession, haunted by the Abraham-Isaac episode in the Old Testament. Ban the Marquis de Sade and you will also have to ban the Bible. No more Academy nudes, no more stocking advertisements, no women (except if Islamically shrouded) in the streets of cities. No *Hamlet*, no *Macbeth*. There would then, because of the outlawing of the reasonable catharsis of art, be far more Moors Murders.

This sounds like a total rejection of the arguments for censorship, and, so far as the State is concerned, it is meant to be. Only a fool would inflame an unbalanced personality with books and pictures of sexual violence (a fool or someone absolutely—theologically—evil). A reputable publisher will not put his business at risk by selling books which are recognizably—to the normal, anyway—instruments of erotic stimulation: his list is limited to the artistic and the didactic. Hard-core pornography is normally censored by price. The reasonable elements of the community (I mean the community, not the State) contrive to preserve the weaker from excessive stimulation. The evil and unbalanced are in a minority, and the culture of the majority may not be emasculated because of a few aberrants.

Sometimes pornography gets through even the most refined net. This, I believe, happened with a novel called *The Night Clerk*, which won, inexplicably, the last Prix Formentor. One's anger at this had nothing to do with the danger of corruption: it was the categorical anger that saw an instrument of stimulation masquerading as a work of art. The publishers of *Ulysses, The Well of Loneliness, Lady Chatterley's Lover, The Image and the Search* and *Last Exit to Brooklyn* are reputable, and always were: it is at least conceivable that they are better qualified for the exercise of censorship than jurymen who may know nothing of literature, or even magistrates whose idea of a daring modern yarn is something by Marie Corelli.

The best argument against external censorship by church or state is still Juvenal's: *"Quis custodiet ipsos custodes?"* Why should a grocer-alderman consider himself qualified to prevent a student of Joyce from seeing the film of *Ulysses?* Why should a nonspecialist and perhaps even only partly literate jury, directed by a judge untrained in aesthetics, prevent an honest inquirer from learning about the sexual mores of Brooklyn perverts? Why should a Maynooth priest seek to protect Irish morals by proscribing the novels of Edna O'Brien or, for that matter, Anthony Burgess? Our souls are ultimately our own, and it is only to God that we pray not to be led into temptation.

The recent judgment on *Last Exit to Brooklyn* is a sorry and disquieting affair. It is not only a question of the inability of the law to encompass matters of aesthetics—a question, incidentally, which Sinyavsky made the basis of his defence in the trial of himself and Daniel in February 1966. It is a matter of the law's apparent inability to cope with the semantics of its own terms of reference. The act under which the book was tried condemns whatever is conducive to concupiscence and lewdness; the judgment seems to confuse such conducement with what can only be termed an appalled and near-Swiftian representation of sexual violence and perversion. The book is what the enlightened American judgment on *Ulysses* called "emetic." To be sick may not be pleasant, but there is no law against making people sick. And there is not much common sense at work when a dose of mustard-and-water can be confused with a pinch of cantharides. Our would-be censors ought to try a little common sense when the next honest work of literature comes up to earn suppression through excess of human concern. All novelists must feel uneasy now. It might be anybody's book. It might be mine.

Harry Levin

The Unbanning of the Books

WHEN I WAS A FRESHMAN AT HARVARD, A CAMBRIDGE BOOK-seller was jailed for selling a copy of Joyce's *Ulysses* to a customer who turned out to be an agent from the Watch and Ward Society of Massachusetts. Such measures, drastic as they may seem, were not enough to preserve the innocence of literate Americans. During a previous summer, like hundreds of others, I had bought my copy from the publisher Sylvia Beach at her little Paris bookshop on the rue de l'Odéon. To pack it wrapped in laundry and smuggle it past the U.S. customs inspectors, thereby involving ourselves in what was called "booklegging," gave us an easy thrill of complicity with the embattled author and his courageous champions. Four years afterward in 1933, the time of Repeal, the ban on *Ulysses* was lifted. The critical decision, which opened the way for an American edition the following year, was handed down by Judge John M. Woolsey of the U.S. District Court for Southern New York.

That incisive opinion acted as a great watershed, since it reversed the trend of earlier opinions and would be frequently cited in later ones. Specifically, books had been condemned on the basis of passages which sounded offensive when taken out of context and without concern for the author's design. Moreover, the determining question had been, in the reverberating phraseology of the so-called Hicklin Rule, whether the reading of such books would tend to "deprave and corrupt" those into whose hands they were likely to fall, regardless of—or rather, with special regard for—their immaturity. Some of the world's acknowledged classics could be adjudged obscene, and had been, by such procedures. The freedom to read had been abridged for educated adults because a mooted book might fall into the hands of children. Mr. Podsnap's cautionary principle of Victorian morality had become a legal criterion: "Would it bring a blush into the cheek of a young person?"

Instead of the *jeune fille* as final arbiter of the book's effect, Judge Woolsey proposed "what the French would call *l'homme moyen sensuel.*" The law now seems to recognize this concept of the normal adult reader, "a person with average sex instincts," as the counterpart to its "reasonable man" in matters of practical judgment. As for the dishing up of salacious tidbits carefully chosen to nauseate the courtroom, it is now general practice to consider a work of literature as a whole. Taking the trouble to master Joyce's demanding technique, Judge Woolsey found that *Ulysses* presented modern life in elaborate cross section. Its round of daily activities included the library and the concert hall as well as the bedroom and bathroom. Sexual and other bodily functions occupied no larger place than they might in ordinary lives.

The same extenuation could scarcely be urged for *Lady Chatterley's Lover,* which is overwhelmingly preoccupied with sex. That may help to explain why it remained unpublishable in the United States until 1959 and in Great Britain until 1961, a generation after Lawrence's death. Nor could it be argued by his admirers that this intense last novel was his masterpiece, as *Ulysses* was Joyce's. Obviously, D. H. Lawrence was less the dispassionate artist than James Joyce. But Lawrence was a passionate moralist, who preached his unorthodox message with evangelical fervor, and therein lay the strength that could be rallied to his support when *Lady Chatterley's Lover* went on trial at the Old Bailey. The intervening years had seen drastic changes, if not in sexual habits or morals, then in the frankness and sincerity with which they could be publicly discussed. The voice in the wilderness, while losing none of its militant solemnity, had been amplified into a posthumous cause.

The very name of the case, *Regina v. Penguin,* suggesting as it does a chapter from *Alice in Wonderland,* aptly announced the procession of church dignitaries, lady dons, schoolmasters, librarians, editors, critics, and publicists who took the witness stand. Penguin soon was circulating 200,000 paperbacks at three shillings and sixpence apiece. In retrospect it seems particularly significant that, unlike other trials which have led to the unbanning of suppressed books, this one had been decided by a jury. The prosecution, trying to extend the obsolete Hicklin Rule, had asked the jurymen: "Is it a book that you would even wish your wife or your servants to read?" And the defense had taken that point by reminding them that they lived in a democratic society, characterized by equal rights for women, the decline of the servant class, and the production of Penguin Books. The vindication of *Lady Chatterley's Lover* spoke, like the novel itself, for the social as well as the sexual revolution.

Regina v. Penguin Books Limited was the test case under the new Obscene Publications Act of 1959. Thus it rounded off a cycle, the century of the Hicklin Rule, which in turn had been based on Lord Campbell's Obscene Publications Act of 1857. By a coincidence which may be worth noting, that year likewise marked the interdiction of *Madame Bovary,* and it is certainly worth noting that Flaubert was acquitted. The idea of suppressing literature on suspicion of its demoralizing potentialities is at least as old as Plato. Through the course of history, however, censorship has mainly been exerted against religious heresy or political subversion. The censor as guardian of private morality is essentially a mid-Victorian figure. His period of dominance in Anglo-American culture was unconscionably prolonged, with such untoward results as can be read in the lives and works of Hardy, George Moore, and Shaw, or of Whitman, Mark Twain, and Dreiser.

The brilliant writers of the early twentieth century grew up in an atmosphere of libertarian protest against what Lawrence called "the censor-morons"—whom we might recognize, under a courtlier phrase, as H. L. Mencken's *"virtuosi* of virtue." Joyce and Lawrence, each in his unique way, could realize their talents only through expatriation. Both *Ulysses* and *Lady Chatterley's Lover* could have been first published only in France, where tradition has been especially tolerant to books printed in English and destined for illegal export. The judicial decisions that naturalized these two novels into the body of English literature, all too belatedly, had to square them with prevailing moral standards. Judge Woolsey concluded his decision with an epigrammatic flourish, by stating that the effect of *Ulysses,* while somewhat emetic, was not aphrodisiac. *Lady Chatterley's Lover* could not be so easily exonerated from the charge of undue eroticism; but, given its preoccupation, it is clearly a tract for reform.

The volume that comes next on our shelf of literary contraband, though it has also been legitimatized by the courts, takes us into more problematic areas of discussion. *Tropic of Cancer* has not the high dedication of the two books we smuggled in before it. Indeed, its utter laxity is a source of its appeal to a later generation which, perhaps, may feel more kinship with underground man than with the intransigent intellectual. Nor does the stature of Henry Miller begin to compare with that of Joyce or Lawrence; yet his critical reputation has profited from the confusions that have surrounded theirs. When compared with Joyce, as George Orwell pointed out in his farsighted essay "Inside the Whale," Miller hardly seems an artist at all. As a would-be moralist he stands at the opposite pole from Lawrence, who would have been more outraged than anyone else by the loveless fornications of *Tropic of Cancer*.

Insofar as there are degrees of vulnerability to attacks from more conventional moralists, this is a harder book to defend than its predecessors. Yet Miller has an undeniable talent, a kind of raffish gusto, as a braggart storyteller in the picaresque mode. While his monologue drifts along the gutters of Paris, it turns up some memorable flotsam. Unfortunately, and increasingly in his other work, this authentic vein of pungent humor is adulterated by messianic rhapsodies— *Leaves of Grass* gone to seed—which prove more embarrassing. Nevertheless, the seriousness of their intentions cannot be denied. Consequently, in 1961, when the attorney general of Massachusetts sought to ban the recent American edition of *Tropic of Cancer,* several critics were on hand to testify on its behalf. The case was heard in the superior court, where the judge decreed the book to be "obscene, indecent, and impure." That decree was subsequently reversed by the Supreme Judicial Court of the Commonwealth.

When I reread this decision and see my testimony quoted, I must confess that my feelings are somewhat mixed. I had ventured to say, in effect, that the book's predominant mood was "one of sexual revulsion," and that its self-conscious morbidity reflected a sense of cultural decadence. Of course I stand by this view, and feel honored that some of the justices evidently concurred with it. But I cannot help wondering whether the book or I would have had their approval if the suggested line of interpretation had emphasized the joys of the flesh. The puritanical implication is that a writer may concern himself with sex if he treats it as a bad thing, or so long as his treatment of it is emetic rather than aphrodisiac. As a matter of fact, my fellow witnesses found Miller's outlook healthier than I did. One of them even introduced a fascinating comparison between *Tropic of Cancer* and *Huckleberry Finn.*

My colleagues, whom I respect, may conceivably be right. In any case, as professors of literature, we are used to critical disagreements. I trust that the judges allow for this variance, and do not take our personal opinions for absolute verities simply because we are consulted as "experts" offering "evidence as to the literary, cultural, or educational character" of the writings in question. What surprised me in the *Tropic of Cancer* affair was that no evidence could be admitted from psychiatrists and social workers. Similarly, in *Regina v. Penguin,* where the court listened so patiently to schoolmistresses and theologians, the defense could get no hearing for doctors and "people who deal with those who are sexually depraved or corrupted"—granted that such expertise is hard to come by, and that the behavioral sciences are far from exact in their application. We are all left in the dark on the crucial point: the actual impact of the alleged means of corruption.

With regard to obscenity, the law has modified itself so extensively in recent years that the interested layman is bewildered, and not less so when he finds himself suddenly called upon as an expert by the courts. Bewilderments are bound to arise from questions which lie open at both ends; and though a book is an objective artifact, the intent of its author is subjective, and so is its effect upon the reader. As the Director of Public Prosecutions said in discussing the Obscene Publications Act, " 'Intent' is a difficult word." There

is even a school of formalistic critics which would rule out
"the intentional fallacy." Judge Woolsey supplied his colleagues on the bench with another epigram, which they have
used to test the purity of a writer's motives, when he spoke
of "dirt for dirt's sake." The late Justice Frankfurter, characteristically asking for more precision, suggested that the
phrase be changed to "dirt for money's sake."

But to speak of dirt is to beg a subtle question. And if the
practice of writing for money is generally approved, why
should it be specially enjoined against when the subject matter happens to be the important matter of sex? Is it because
of the possible effect? Then we shift our ground, and the
lawyers begin to talk about provoking lustful thoughts or appealing to prurient interest. Ordinarily we praise a writer
when, in dealing with any other subject, he manages to convey sensations and stimulate reactions. Advertisers vie with
one another, using a directly visual stimulus, to inject an
erotic flavor into the most irrelevant situations. We cannot
walk through our day without encountering dozens of random excitations which, if we are healthy, ought to arouse
our susceptibilities. "A state of mind is not enough," Mr.
Justice Douglas has written; "it is the relationship of that
state of mind to overt action that would seem to be critical."

It is humbling to realize how little is known about the nature of that relationship, and how widely the trains of speculation diverge. Literature is full of stories that demonstrate
—and possibly exaggerate—the influence of literature on
behavior, such as Dante's poignant example of Paolo and
Francesca, who became lovers after reading a romance together. Specialists in children's problems earnestly and end-
lessly debate over comic books: whether they are a major
cause of juvenile delinquency or a valid inoculation against
it. Classicists and psychoanalysts alike believe in catharsis,
the notion that the mind can be purged of its antisocial
tendencies by participating in vicarious passions. Tragedy
has been exhibiting crimes on the stage for centuries, and its
aftereffects are usually regarded as elevating rather than con-

ducive to further crime. Books that dwell on sexual episodes might be just as likely to relieve tensions as to incite lewd and lascivious conduct.

At all events, we must have broader experience, keener observation, and more systematic investigation before we can make confident assumptions regarding how a given piece of reading matter would affect an unforeseen variety of readers. It may be that the Kinsey Institute, which has assembled an impressive library of erotica, will carry its researches into this limbo and bring us back some antiseptic answers. In the meantime, the reading public has been enjoying an unprecedented latitude. The battles for Joyce (inclusion of sex as part of the all-round picture), Lawrence (emphasis on sex as a means of salvation), and Miller (obsession with sex as a nihilistic gesture) have opened the floodgates. After *Ulysses, Lady Chatterley's Lover,* and *Tropic of Cancer,* what then? Irreversibly the progression moves on, impelled by its own momentum, a sheer need for the next revelation to outstrip the last one. Having exploited the themes of normal sexuality, it seeks new disclosures by turning to perversion and inversion.

Censorship has backed down with less and less struggle, as Vladimir Nabokov's *Lolita* or William Burroughs' *Naked Lunch* has bridged the rapid transition from the Parisian bookleggers to a New York imprimatur—and, what is more, to an open market in Boston. Nabokov would be an exception in any grouping, a displaced mandarin from a more elegant age, and his flirtation with vice is merely another whim of his idiosyncrasy. Burroughs continues Miller's sodden bohemianism well into its gangrenous stage. He finds his material by wallowing deeper and deeper, and relies on drugs to give it an imaginative lift. Yet even *Naked Lunch* pays tribute to moralism in a preface and in an appended article written for the *British Journal of Addiction.* Therein Burroughs observes the convention of gallows literature, where the condemned man edifies the crowd by warning them against his particular fate. So Nabokov, tongue in cheek as usual, palms off *Lolita* as a psychiatric case history. The quest for sensation has been approaching the line between serious literature and pornography, if indeed that borderline is still discernible. Joyce and Lawrence both drew it very sharply, since their artistic integrity depended upon it. "Genuine pornography is almost always underworld," Lawrence could write; "it doesn't come into the open." Manifestly, we live in another epoch. The notorious *Memoirs of a Woman of Pleasure,* which has won greater notoriety as *Fanny Hill,* earned John Cleland a reprimand from the Privy Council when he brought it out in the year of *Tom Jones.* Its transatlantic distribution led in 1821 to the first American suppression for obscenity. Notwithstanding, it has gained and held a place in Anglo-American culture, quite properly a surreptitious place among bookdealers' *curiosa.* Lately it has been brought out from under the counter and commended to a waiting world by Nabokov's publisher, the reputable old firm that published Washington Irving and Herman Melville.

In the light of these developments, we can appreciate the historic irony of the announcement by Maurice Girodias, head of the Olympia Press and original publisher of the once-prohibited books by Miller, Nabokov, and Burroughs. His remarkable list includes Samuel Beckett, Lawrence Durrell, and other English-writing luminaries of the current international twilight, along with certain titles which might still be classified somewhere as "hard-core pornography." M. Girodias has declared his intention of moving his operations from Paris to the United States, as soon as he can disentangle them from his present difficulties with the French government. We have come a long way from the days of Sylvia Beach; and so has France, presumably, in the other direction. M. Girodias has reason to envy the Grove Press of New York, which has been so successful in domesticating many of the works that are giving him trouble, notably the English translation of Genet's *Notre Dame des Fleurs.*

Jean Genet is a writer of unquestioned power, whose style alone would set his books apart from the pornographic confessions they often resemble, and from those American novels and stories which have recently been putting us into close touch with the homosexual demimonde. Yet it would be uncritical to think that Genet was not obscene, though his verbose apologist, Jean-Paul Sartre, argues the contrary: obscenity is the stance for Genet's virulent critique of modern society. In this respect, as in others, he is an heir to the Marquis de Sade, that pariah of the eighteenth century who has become a culture hero today, and whose most provocative writings have recently been handsomely republished by the Grove Press. Since Mr. Justice Brennan has ruled in the Roth case of 1957 that "all ideas having even the slightest redeeming social importance" are entitled to constitutional protection, the needle's eye would seem to be large enough for the passage of such camels.

Not much room has been left for any working definition of pornography; its hard core has been softened, at any rate. Its etymological meaning, "writing about prostitution," should have some bearing on *Fanny Hill* (banned by the Massachusetts court that unbanned *Tropic of Cancer*), where every page invites what Judge Woolsey long ago called "the leer of the sensualist." But a book like *Candy* works both sides of the street by offering itself as a parody of the pornographic genre (pornography being itself a parody of more serious fiction). Rarities formerly locked in the librarians' Inferno are available in paperback, sometimes in competing editions where the sanctions of copyright fail to apply. It could be suspected that, whereas the oldfashioned censor-morons confounded art with pornography, we are now being invited to accept pornography as art. However, the old distinctions no longer serve. Those who might once have been stigmatized as purveyors of smut, "dirt for money's sake," are hailed as benefactors of civil liberties, *virtuosi* of virtue at a profit.

Established   novelists   do   their   best—and   worst—to keep up with the subterranean movement, and to keep on the best-seller lists, by providing their characters with more and more detailed bedroom histories. Norman Mailer asserted in 1959 that sex was "perhaps the last remaining frontier of the novel which has not been exhausted by the nineteenth and early twentieth century novelists." One might have assumed that this territory was not altogether virgin before *An American Dream,* but Mailer is amply justified in his pioneering metaphor. From its first emergence, with the breakthrough of the middle class into literature, the novel has been explicitly committed to the enlargement of human experience. Its great practitioners have all been realists, in the sense that they had to cut through conventions and fight against hypocrisies while striving to capture some segment of reality which has hitherto gone unexpressed. Hence they scandalized the authorities of their day, who retorted with repressive tactics.

Flaubert, Dostoevsky, even the Brontës—no less than Lawrence, Joyce, and their successors—all arrived by *succès de scandale.* Invariably, contemporaries are shocked by innovation in the arts and commonly accuse the innovators of being sensation-mongers, which from time to time they must be. But the shock wears off with habituation, and what is no longer new can thereupon be judged by whether or not it seems true. It was shocking to see the forbidden monosyllables in print while *Ulysses* was proscribed, though they might not have offended in masculine conversation or in feminine stream of consciousness. Nowadays we have merely to ask ourselves whether or not they fit into the fictional contexts in which they so freely appear. The convention of using asterisks or dashes seems as quaint as Ernest Hemingway's substitution of the word "obscenity" for the Spanish oaths in *For Whom the Bell Tolls.* Profanity derives its peculiar force from the violation of a taboo; expletives become meaningless once the taboos lose their hold.

When the Berkeley students shouted dirty words from a public platform, they confirmed the proprieties against which they were protesting. If speech were completely free, no words would bring a blush to a young person's cheek or raise the eyebrows of an older one. As with the language, so with the contents of books. Descriptions of sexual intimacy, if we get used to reading them, ought to provoke no special titillation. We should be able to take them or leave them, depending on whether they carry honest conviction. When everything has been said, we can focus on how it is said. We may still need safeguards for the immature; but for adults so much is already permitted that not much can consistently be excluded. Our freedom to read, as guaranteed by the law, is virtually complete. Free speech and due process, the First and Fourteenth Amendments to the Constitution as reinterpreted by Justice Brennan, reaffirm the humanism of Terence: "I am a human being, and therefore consider nothing human alien to me."

Accordingly, when writers are allowed to write anything they please and publishers to put it into circulation, then the great responsibility for discrimination rests with the reader. Art in itself may be neither moral nor immoral, as Oscar Wilde insisted; but since we are potentially both, the courts stand ready to correct our overt immorality. Meanwhile, it remains for us to determine the uses of art. If we abandon censorship, we depend all the more imperatively upon criticism. If we agree that books are neither dirty nor clean, we must be sure to remember that they are bad or good, and must not be distracted into ignoring that difference. After all, it has never been too difficult to tell a potboiler from a work of art, and it should be even simpler with potboilers that concentrate upon sex to the point of monotony. To criticize them is to discriminate between artistic imagination and autistic fantasy. One of the wholesome results of our hard-won candor is that it could end by driving the pornographers out of business.

Vivian Mercier

Master Percy and/or
Lady Chatterley

THE SOCIAL CONTEXT

MY FIRST CONTACT WITH PORNOGRAPHY IN THE SENSE OF WRIT-
ing "intended to arouse sexual desire" also provided my first
contact with a living manuscript tradition. Someone at my
boys' boarding school in Ireland got a letter from a friend
containing a transcription of an erotic poem, supposedly
by Lord Byron. I now forget the title, but the poem gave
an idealized yet explicit description of sexual intercourse
between a handsome boy of nineteen and a beautiful girl
of sixteen. I think I copied it out in longhand, and I cer-

tainly knew most of its perhaps fifty lines by heart at one time, but all that remains now is the most innocuous of its undistinguished octosyllabic couplets:

The girl, methought, was just sixteen,
While he three summers more had seen.

If Byron indeed wrote it, then he was probably a Harrow schoolboy himself at the time.

To understand the powerful effect of such a basically conventional poem upon me and my contemporaries—we had all just reached or were reaching puberty—one has to remember the context. This was the first piece of literature we had ever seen that spoke approvingly of extramarital sex—or approvingly of sex at all, unless we had already found our way to the Song of Solomon in the Bible. Compared with the alternatives open to us—"dirty" stories that usually befouled or belittled sex, and schoolboy homosexuality—this "pornography" was almost entirely wholesome in its effect. Of course it incited us to masturbation, but we all masturbated more or less regularly anyway; no doubt the description of the boy meant more to some of us than that of the girl, but personally I found nourishment for my heterosexual fantasies, which had been rather anemic up to that point: I had never seen a mature woman or girl naked below the waist, and I doubt whether most of my classmates had even had my luck in catching at least hasty glimpses of lovely bosoms. (A cousin of my father's ran a girls' boarding school and took me on as a boarder when I was not quite nine, while my father was recovering from a severe illness.)

A similar poem, entitled "A Simple Village Maiden," reached us a year or two later; as I recall, it was somewhat less idealized than the other one. Later still, someone had copies of an American pulp magazine, *College Humor,* which contained fairly explicit descriptions of necking and petting scenes. What fascinated us was tongue-kissing, something we had never tried with girls in the vacations; we

found it hard to believe that such a seemingly disgusting operation could be pleasurable. Finally, somebody rented a serious sex manual from a stall in Smithfield Market, Belfast,
that we read partly as pornography, but I don't think any of
the "variations" so antiseptically discussed by its author
found their way into my fantasies.

After eight years of all-male boarding schools, I entered
Trinity College, Dublin, at seventeen; since even J. P. Don-
leavy's uninhibited heroes seem wary of the coeds there, it is
perhaps not surprising that an only child like myself,
brought up almost entirely apart from girls, should never
have had a love affair with a Trinity girl. Some of my classmates were more enterprising, but I didn't fully lose my virginity until I was almost twenty-one, and then with an English girl. I read a good many plain-spoken classics of English
and French literature in my undergraduate years, but I had
only two contacts with "hard-core" pornography in all that
time. A classmate brought back from Europe a series of utterly explicit photographs of couples engaged in various heterosexual activities: they might have been so many anatomical drawings for all the desire they aroused in me. The men
and women were ugly, apparently chosen for the size of their
genitals to the exclusion of all other criteria. I could no
more imagine myself doing what they were doing than I
could identify with the sensualists in the obscene poems of
Martial that I had painstakingly translated for myself at age
sixteen or seventeen.

The privilege of revealing to me some of the potentialities
of my own sexual nature was reserved for a crudely written,
abominably printed slab of commercial pornography bearing
the preposterous title *Master Percy's Adventures in the Family Circle and Outside*. I haven't the slightest intention of relating any of those adventures, which began with a lascivious
maid-servant, continued with an emancipated aunt,
progressed—if that is the right word—by way of "my
lovely mother" to the gamekeeper's wife and ten-year-old
daughter. After thus avenging Sir Clifford Chatterley Bt., Mas-

ter Percy found male allies to participate in the multiple orgies which seem obligatory in the later chapters of such
works, but by this time I had lost interest in him. Suffice it
to say that I had pieced out the anonymous author's imper-
fections with my thoughts and considerably enriched the
content of my sexual fantasies.

In the prime of life, some of our fantasies, sexual and otherwise, become facts; there were times when I had reason to
be grateful to Master Percy, and perhaps one or two of the
women I have loved would have been grateful to him too if
they had suspected his sub-literary existence. But it is in periods of sexual deprivation—to which the young and the
old are far more subject than those in their prime—that
males, at any rate, are likely to reap psychological benefit
from pornography. Am I mistaken, or have I read somewhere that geriatricians occasionally prescribe the reading of
it to their patients? At any rate, it seems to be axiomatic that
most of those who have lost all interest in sex have also lost
interest in living.

PERILS OF PORNOGRAPHY

In retrospect, my encounters with pornography seem to have
been preponderantly benign, but they did make me aware of
potential dangers. There must surely be a percentage of
males whose only sex outlet has become the reading of pornography accompanied by masturbation. In many cases,
where the fantasies catered to involve, e.g., sadism or incest,
this situation may be socially desirable. I assume, rightly or
wrongly, that a person who has become aware of these tendencies in himself through contact with pornography will be
better able to cope with them than someone who has unconsciously repressed them; I also assume that pornography cannot cause such tendencies but simply reveals what is already
latent. If there is any research that conclusively refutes these
assumptions, I have not heard of it. It even seems unlikely
that male or female homosexuals should first become aware

of their tendencies through reading pornography, though they might learn from it how to satisfy their desires. One very real danger inherent in the wish-fulfilling nature of pornography is that it may create unrealizable expectations. Montaigne humorously complained that women were doomed to disappointment if they believed in the huge male organs to be seen drawn on walls. Far more misleading are the pornographic conventions that represent all partners as always willing and all acts of intercourse as ending in simultaneous orgasm. These conventions not only arouse false hopes: they make no allowance for the infinite variety of human sexuality. All too often, a pornographic work guarantees one specific method of arousal—doubtless an obsession of the author—as sure-fire in all situations, whereas every woman needs to be wooed differently.

Furthermore, males who hope to use pornography as a stimulus in normal sex activity may find it has an opposite effect. Premature ejaculation is an obvious possibility; less obvious, perhaps, is impotence. Indulgence in fantasy may exhaust or defuse the libido so that it fails to respond to reality. Recall the old story of the rather refined young man who preferred sex dreams to visiting brothels because he met a much nicer type of girl that way. To sum up: pornography may be valuable as a substitute for normal sex or for antisocial sex activities, but as an adjunct to sex it may create more problems than it solves.

PORNOGRAPHY AND ART

One need not be a dogmatic Freudian to believe that Sex is inseparable from Art. How much great lyric poetry would be left if we banished all the love poems? Renoir is reputed to have said that he painted his warm-blooded nudes with his penis. Two such profound tragic writers as Sophocles and Tolstoy confessed with shame that they were subject to sexual desire after their eightieth birthdays. James Joyce said that he inherited from his father "an extravagant licentious disposition (out of which, however, the greater part of any talent I may have springs). . . ." Anyone at all familiar with modern poetry is aware of W. B. Yeats's epigram, "The Spur," written in his seventies. In it, he refuses to apologize for the large part played by "lust and rage" in his later poetry:

They were not such a plague when I was young
What else have I to spur me into song?

As the content of the work of Sophocles or Tolstoy shows, sex may be almost entirely sublimated in great art. Or it may be represented directly and yet with the kind of artistic "distancing" that rules out pornography. Perhaps no reader has ever experienced sexual arousal even on first acquaintance with Yeats's sonnet, "Leda and the Swan." On the other hand, the average male will have to read Molly Bloom's inner monologue, which forms the last episode of Joyce's *Ulysses,* two or three times before it loses its capacity to arouse him sexually. The point is that when his excitement has at last been overcome, he will find the entire episode still more interesting than it was before: crammed to bursting with psychological insights, visual imagery, and intricate aural rhythm. "Hard-core" pornography, on the other hand, contains nothing else of interest when once its power to arouse has been exhausted. Drs. Eberhard and Phyllis Kronhausen have drawn the dividing line between "erotic realism" and pornography with great skill in their admirable *Pornography and the Law* (New York: Ballantine Books, 1959); I hope this work is now available in hard covers.

But things have moved so fast since 1959 that the Kronhausens' book could now be reissued complete with all the "taboo" words for which they felt compelled to substitute clinical terms or circumlocutions. The constant appearance of these four-letter words, not only in best-selling fiction but in the news reports of at least some "family" newspapers, may eventually compel us to redraft the boundary between pornography and realism. The Kronhausens rightly pointed out how characteristic of hard-core pornography was "the *quantity* of taboo words used." They might have added, however, that this is not necessarily characteristic of pornography in all languages, nor even of pornography in English in all centuries. An obvious but rarely made point about the notorious eighteenth-century classic of pornography, *Fanny Hill,* is that it contains not one single "dirty" word. As we know, even the middle classes were not particularly mealy-mouthed in England in the eighteenth century: perhaps taboo words did not become an essential part of the pornographic conventions until Victorian days.

Twentieth-century French commercial pornography— admittedly I have not examined very much of this— seems to go to extraordinary lengths to avoid the use of obscene words. The writers of it appear to take a competitive delight in finding witty circumlocutions or fantastic pseudo-Freudian images to replace the plain French for their subject matter. One might suspect that this is done to avoid the penalties of the law and to ensure that the books and magazines may be safely sold over the counter. But the real reason is surely that the primitive words have lost all their power in French, so that the primary meaning of *con* is no longer "cunt" but "dumb bastard" and that of *foutre* is no longer "fuck" but "damn it." This view can readily be supported by a look at the innumerable imaginative synonyms to be found in a good dictionary of *argot.*

What about French eighteenth-century pornography, then? Does it revel in obscene words, supplying the converse to *Fanny Hill?* I'm afraid I have never done the research necessary to answer this question. Certainly much French writing that our ancestors regarded as pornographic is far too artistic to deserve that slur. Only recently did I look into the work of the supposedly diabolical Crébillon *fils.* If his *La nuit et le moment (The Night and the Moment)* be representative of his work as a whole, he has been greatly maligned. He does arouse the reader sexually, of course: one would be justly disappointed if a conversation between a

man and woman in the latter's bedroom did not have that effect. But, again, obscene words are never employed—not
even, I think, the standard French expression for "to have
orgasm," *jouir,* which primarily means "to enjoy." Yet everything is said: past sexual episodes are described in fairly full
detail and with relish. The psychological conventions of this
sophisticated eroticism are quite subtle: it is accepted that a
woman cannot have orgasm unless she feels a certain degree
of emotional involvement with her partner; on the other
hand, in order to justify that involvement, she would like to
be convinced that the man in his turn feels a sentimental at-
tachment to her. In a social circle where everyone sooner or
later ends up in bed with everyone else, it may be hard to
preserve the illusion of romantic love, but these erotic casu-
ists do try. Nothing could be more different from the ruth-
less pursuit of "conquest" in Choderlos de Laclos's *Les liai-
sons dangereuses*—a single novel on which far too many
generalizations about French eighteenth-century eroticism
have been based. The Kinsey Report on *Sexual Behavior in
the Human Female* indicated that few American women are
aroused by hard-core pornography. One wonders whether an
English-language equivalent of the younger Crébillon might
not have more appeal for them. I forget whether the Kinsey
questionnaire asked about the effects on the feminine libido
of "romantic" fiction. A recent British study indicates that
married women in Great Britain read romantic novels more
often than unmarried women do. Apparently British husbands
can appease their wives' sexual appetites more easily than they
can satisfy those ladies' yearnings for Romance with a capital
"R."
    The study of pornography in even its most crudely com-
mercial forms does offer certain lessons to the critic of literature or the fine arts. Above all, like any study of popular,
subliterary forms such as the Western story, it teaches the
immense power of convention. The Kronhausens have described the basic structure of obscene books and all their
major conventions with real critical flair. Some of these conventions, such as the permissive attitude toward incest—

explicitly advertised in the full title of *Master Percy's Adventures*—are very readily explained by Freudian theory. Others perhaps seem a matter of common sense: for instance, the convention, taken for granted by the Kronhausens, that the adult male and female genitalia and pubic hair are to be described as esthetically pleasing to the senses of sight and smell. This prettifying convention seems in keeping with the unrealistic nature of pornography as a whole, but it hardly matches the uglifying convention that insists upon copious emission of seminal and vaginal fluid, not to mention the emphasis on taboo words.

Japanese art seems so intent on stylizing and idealizing the visual beauty of landscapes, human figures, and buildings that it is startling to find the genitalia in Japanese erotic art stylized in the opposite sense. Not only are both male and female organs greatly enlarged but their details are presented in such a way as to emphasize wrinkles, fleshiness, and hairiness. No humorous or satirical undercutting of sex appears to be intended, for the rest of the picture is usually of considerable visual beauty and often seems imbued with "serious" emotion. Philip Rawson, in *Erotic Art of the East* (New York: G. P. Putnam's Sons, 1968), insists that although "the Japanese convention often seems to Europeans grotesque . . . to Japanese eyes it is not grotesque, but normal." His explanation of the convention sounds plausible: ". . . in real life the Japanese have been so casually familiar with the appearance of the genitals as a normal part of the naked human body that to raise these familiar objects to the status of an emotive and sensuous focus in a work of art demands dramatic treatment." Rawson also suggests that the Japanese habit of communal nude bathing explains why the participants in pornographic scenes are often almost fully clothed.

If the Japanese viewed their stylization of the genitals as grotesque or comic, the *shunga* scrolls and prints would be virtually useless as sexual stimuli. We often make the mistake of lumping pornography and "dirty jokes" together, but in fact they stand at opposite poles, or nearly so. The effect of sex jokes, insofar as it is not purely intellectual and asexual, is to release sexual tensions, rather than to build them up toward a climax as pornography does. The profoundest comic literature takes as its subject matter the most serious, the "biggest" things in life—death, religion, sex—and proceeds to cut them down to size. It may seem ridiculous to speak of reverence in relation to pornography, yet the Kronhausens rightly detect survivals of ancient phallic worship in some modern commercial pornography.

An extraordinary aura of reverence, incidentally, surrounds the name of the Marquis de Sade in certain *avantgarde* circles today: our contemporary satirists are missing a custom-made target for irreverence. The difficulty, of course, lies in finding a way to parody the Marquis's heavy-breathing style without lapsing into pornography oneself. It might be easier in the end to out-Herod Herod in the manner of Swift's *A Modest Proposal*. For instance, why bother with women who are disgustingly healthy? Why not start in with an invalid, crippled woman? "My dear Marquis, having intercourse with a woman suffering from this disease seems to me preferable to making love to a corpse that is still warm; unfortunately, unlike you, I have not had the latter pleasure and lack a basis for comparison."

MEDIA

The "new freedom" with regard to sex in American life and art is a sometime thing at best. I have been confining myself almost exclusively to the medium of print thus far, yet this in itself is a vast field encompassing several different standards of permissiveness. Almost anything can appear in book form these days, as Grove Press seems determined to prove, but many serious magazines and newspapers exercise almost as great a degree of self-censorship as they ever did. In women's magazines, almost any deviation from traditional norms of sexual morality may be advocated, almost any anatomical detail of sex named and commented on—provided that it appears under the heading of nonfiction. Fiction and poetry (if any), however, appear to hew to the same line as they did thirty years ago. Much the same is true of the *Atlantic* and *Harper's*.

I have had personal experience of this anomaly. Two years ago I wrote a mildly erotic poem called "The Trout," which pleases most of the mature men and women I show it to and has even won the approval of a poetry editor or two. But somehow it doesn't get published. The "trout" of the title is clearly a woman, and fishing is a transparent metaphor for intercourse culminating in her orgasm. The big stumbling block seems to be one phrase, "She gulps my bait," which I intended to refer to tongue-kissing but which editors take in a more obscene sense. Even so, the poem does not seem to me basically indecent, and I am sure that if I offered it to the editor of an "underground" periodical, he would reject it as too tame. I wonder how many writers have lately had this experience of falling between two stools, of facing a double standard both of whose poles reject them.

About the range of the new freedom in the performing arts, my own squeamishness forces me to rely mainly on hearsay. I would as soon witness a public beheading as a public copulation. The most "daring" scene I have witnessed in a movie was the stylized, understated scene of masturbation in *The Fox*. This I found undisturbing, because nobody could have supposed for a moment that the actress involved was actually having an orgasm. Female orgasm may manifest itself as anything from the genteel shudder of a lady drinking a nasty medicine to something approximating an epileptic fit, but nobody could have mistaken what the actress did for the performance of a private act in public.

It's possible that I have an unusually strong sense of what constitutes a violation of others' privacy; at any rate, I share the view of the narrator in Frank O'Connor's story "The Man of the World." Having been persuaded by his friend Jimmy to spy on a young married couple going to bed next door, he doesn't see anything salacious, but, as the young wife knelt to pray, he ". . . felt someone else watching us, so that at once we ceased to be the observers and became the observed. And the observed in such a humiliating position that nothing I could imagine our victims doing would have been so degrading." If performers were counterfeiting the sexual act, I probably would feel as bored as I do during a prolonged death scene; if they weren't pretending, I would feel that I had no business to be watching. This attitude of mine is not incompatible with keen enjoyment of the visual aspects of sex in privacy. It may seem excessive to feel this uneasiness about voyeurism while watching films as well as live performances, yet I cannot help believing that many people share my squeamishness.

A "NEW EROTICS"?

Are we making intelligent use of the new freedom of speech about sex, I wonder? True, a number of writers are holding picnics where Joyce and Lawrence and Gide once fought pitched battles, but they're not really adding much to the sum of human happiness. Lawrence would be chagrined, if he came back from the grave, to see what an orgy of commercialism the vindication of *Lady Chatterley's Lover* has made possible. Think of the satirical poems he would write on Playboy Clubs or "bottomless" go-go dancers!

He might be most disappointed, though, by his fellow artists' neglect of the field of sex education. The marriage manuals and all their semipornographic rivals are in the hands of the medical men (or their quack imitators) and of clinical photographers with artistic aspirations worthy of the Sears-Roebuck catalog. Come to think of it, the new illustrated sex manuals whose advertisements arrive in my mail weekly are themselves catalogues—of positions for the sexual act, some of which would strain the agility of an athletic octopus. Whereas all the great Japanese masters of the woodcut, Utamaro and the rest, contributed to the tradition of the *shunga* scrolls, no great Western artist has, to my knowledge, been invited to illustrate a modern *Art of Love*. And if he were, what sort of a text would be provided for him by a Dr. Knock or a Dr. Pangloss?

Not that the literary men have done much to prove their superiority to the clinicians. If I were asked at this very moment to point out a sort of "Intelligent Woman's Guide to Male Sexuality," I could in good conscience mention only one that is centuries old: Montaigne's famous essay "On Some Ve13es of Virgil." Joyce and Lawrence, in their most famous passages on sex, were female impersonators, and if Henry Miller is telling the truth about male sexuality—something that I don't for one moment believe—no intelligent woman should go in for anything but lesbianism. As for Philip Roth, one woman colleague of mine remarked, "He tells me more about masturbation than I think I care to know." No, if such a guide is to be written, it must be done by a wise, humane man who really loves women—someone like Isaac Bashevis Singer, for instance. And who would write the corresponding "Intelligent Man's Guide to Women"? Doris Lessing, perhaps?

The New Erotics would be a blend of art and science, written and illustrated by artists of one sex for the enlightenment of the other; its ultimate effect, I think, would be not only to help the sexes understand each other better but to bring their modes of sexual self-expression closer together. More women would learn to be—or at least to seem—aggressive in the bedroom, thus heightening their own enjoyment qualitatively as well as quantitatively. On the other hand, many men who have had doubts about their masculinity—and perhaps most men have—would learn once for all that if a woman loves and is sure she is loved, she can make bricks without straw.

Where, though, can one learn how to love as distinct from how to be, in Brendan Behan's phrase, a "sex mechanic"? In the family circle, undoubtedly, though not quite in the manner of Master Percy. It is often said that only a child who has been loved by his or her parents can grow up able to love others, yet we all know at least one emotional cripple who is the victim of overlove from one parent or even both. It is probably more important that the child realize his parents love each other, once he is sure that they love him; also he must somehow, consciously or unconsciously, reach an awareness that their relationship is fully sexual. This can be a very difficult task in urban or suburban middle-class families: I remember the delight of a friend of mine, who had the usual stereotype of his mother as loving but straitlaced and virtually sexless, when he overheard her tell another woman that his father was "lovely in bed." This moment of eavesdropping did more for him than a whole library of erotica or marriage manuals could have done. But as long as we are so secretive that our children can only learn such essential truths about us by eavesdropping, pornography will continue to flourish.

Stanley Edgar Hyman

In Defense of Pornography

WHEN JOHN CLELAND'S FANNY HILL WAS OPENLY PUBLISHED IN 1963, as *Memoirs of a Woman of Pleasure,* I decided not to review it. The occasion was serious, but the book was not. Although written as a first-person memoir by a courtesan, it makes little effort to be convincing as female sexual psychology (as, say, Doris Lessing's *The Golden Notebook* is). When the New York State Supreme Court declared Cleland's book to be obscene and forbade its sale and distribution in the state, I changed my mind about reviewing it. If it does nothing else, a review gives me a chance to congratulate

Walter J. Minton, the president of Putnam's, on his courage in publishing *Memoirs of a Woman of Pleasure* and fighting in the courts for his right to do so. I support him unequivocally in those actions. (Putnam's venture, I should add, would have been unlikely without the prior heroism of Barney Rosset and Grove Press in publishing *Lady Chatterley's Lover* and *Tropic of Cancer* and defending them in the courts.)

The same year, the fourth number of Ralph Ginzburg's hardbound quarterly *Eros* was declared obscene by the United States District Court in Philadelphia, along with another of Ginzburg's publications, *The Housewife's Handbook on Selective Promiscuity*, by "Rey Anthony." *Eros* seems to have been banned for a series of color photographs of embraces between a naked Negro man and a naked white girl. Since the embraces are of the most decorous sort, on the order of studying together, I can only conclude that integrated education is the issue, which makes it the responsibility of other specialists. *The Housewife's Handbook*, however, with the Cleland book, raises important questions about censorship.

Memoirs of a Woman of Pleasure seems a good example of pornography according to Judge Woolsey's distinction in the *Ulysses* case: the exploitation of obscenity with salacious intent. Written in 1749, it tells of the sexual adventures of Fanny Hill, which increase in imaginative variety from page to page. The book has set pieces appealing to various deviant impulses: female and male homosexuality (the latter probably added by a later hand), sadism and masochism, necrophilia, voyeurism, and so forth.

The tone of the sexual descriptions is usually rapturous, particularly in regard to orgasm. Cleland's people might be squirting hot fudge sundaes into one another; "the titillating inspersion of balsamic sweets" is a typical description. Otherwise, in contrast to that of later pornography, the book's style is attractive, with an eighteenth-century distinction of language. Cleland uses no vulgar words, preferring glamorous euphemisms: sex organs are "his mighty machine" and "that luscious mouth of nature"; a rear view of a naked girl "gave somewhat the idea of a pink slash in the glossiest white satin."

Ultimately, I think, *Memoirs of a Woman of Pleasure* becomes boring to adults because of the limited possibilities of variation in these events (a fact for which Cleland several times apologizes in the book). When Fanny copulates standing on her head, *Memoirs* becomes ludicrous. The same ludicrous point is reached in *Jou Pu Tuan* (The Prayer Mat of Flesh), a Chinese seventeenth-century pornographic classic by Li Yü, when the hero progresses from going to bed with three women to going to bed with four. (In contemporary pornography, the absurdity of posture and numbers increases alarmingly.)

As *Memoirs* is a good example of pornography, *The Housewife's Handbook on Selective Promiscuity* seems a good example of obscenity, indecent material *without* salacious intent. I think this despite the offensive title, which Mrs. Anthony says she chose herself, and despite the possibility that the book is a fake. I believe it to be honest and authentic, for reasons soon to be given. It is the frank sexual autobiography or case history of a woman in her late thirties. Its revelation, says Albert Ellis in his introduction, is "that sex can actually be fun." I cannot imagine a wilder misstatement. The bald sex scenes are alternated with similarly bald accounts of the author's whitish vaginal discharge when she had a venereal disease, her dropped and protruding uterus in pregnancy, her self-disgust at not knowing whether any given child is husband's or lover's, her constant money trouble, and her inability to get up the payments for a daughter at the Plucky Poodle School (that Plucky Poodle School is one of the details that lead me to think the book authentic). The *Handbook's* true revelation is that sex can often be a pain and a mess.

What the book is most like is those dreary monologues about their troubles that one gets from hotel chambermaids as the penalty for being in the room when they come to clean it. Mrs. Anthony's main trouble is that she discovered clitoral masturbation at nine and has been fixated on it ever since; she has taught her various husbands and lovers to "massage" (her word) her clitoris to bring her to orgasm, and, since she is not much of a lubricator either, they massage her with Vaseline (I wonder how much the Chesebrough Manufacturing Company will appreciate the plug). This is surely of some interest, but any adult reader sexually excited by it must get his kicks oddly.

What makes me think the book authentic is that the language takes sad little stabs at gentility, unduplicatable by any hack or ghost writer. I italicize: "Clint had found the tips of my breasts *anew*"; simultaneous orgasm proved impractical because "it left no one *at the helm, so to speak*"; "he read a *piercingly* lovely poem to me" (it is by Irwin Edman). The book's lengthy recital of the author's opinions about sex in its emotional, institutional, and legal aspects is as inauthentic as her slightly prissy language is authentic; I assume that she got the opinions from the pile of marriage manuals that one of her lovers presented to her.

I am, then, not a very good witness for the defense, since I believe that both books are suppressible under the law. But the law is wrong. Neither book should be banned; in fact no publication should be banned. I realize that this is the quixotic position of Justice Black, who finds censorship of any kind unconstitutional according to the first amendment's clear statement: "Congress shall make no law . . . abridging the freedom of speech, or of the press." With him, I believe that this means exactly what it says, not the more reasonable and limited thing that we have taken it to mean (as we have similarly corrected those Gospel absolutes about turning the other cheek and loving our enemies).

The argument for the censorship of pornography and obscenity is based on the harmful consequences, to the reader and to society, that are alleged to follow from such reading: masturbation, loss of chastity, fornication, perversion and homosexuality, rape and child violation. In regard to masturbation, I do not believe that it requires any such stimulus. As for loss of chastity, I share Jimmy Walker's doubt that anyone ever got seduced by a book, but if two pure young people *were* to read a book and pop into bed as a consequence, I would answer with D. H. Lawrence, "One up to them!" These books may teach and encourage a wider range of heterosexual activity, oral and anal as well as genital, and should be welcomed if they do. I do not believe that they encourage homosexuality or crimes of sexual violence; I think that they discourage the former by assuaging Oedipal guilts, and make the latter less likely through cathartic release.

All this is hypothetical, since no one knows the effects of such reading on behavior. In 1943, Dr. Glenn V. Ramsey published a list in the *American Journal of Psychology* of what had actually proven sexually exciting to 291 young boys. It included sitting in class, taking a shower, sitting in church, urinating, taking tests, finding money, and hearing the national anthem. None of these seem bannable, except perhaps the national anthem.

While John Cleland is not legally allowed to stimulate sexual desire, whole industries—fashion and advertising, perfume and cosmetics—work at it full time. Mrs. Anthony is not allowed to tell our youngsters what it feels like when a woman is sexually satisfied, but a whole literature tells them with impunity what it feels like when a woman is beaten, kicked, burned, stabbed, or shot. The real corrupter of our youth is sadism, not sex, as that pioneer G. Legman argued in *Love & Death* in 1949, but even here censorship seems inadvisable.

If there were bad consequences of the abolition of censorship, they might be outweighed by the good consequences. Ruth Benedict's classic study, "Continuities and Discontinuities in Cultural Conditioning," in *Psychiatry* in 1938, shows that adolescence is so great a crisis in our culture because our culture is discontinuous, and the adolescent must painfully unlearn one set of standards and learn their opposite.

In regard to sex, we expect a sexless child and a sexually uninhibited adult. As Mrs. Benedict shows, many of our adults
cannot "unlearn the wickedness or the dangerousness of
sex." "It is not surprising," she adds, "that in such a society
many individuals fear to use behavior which has up to that
time been under a ban and trust instead, though at great
psychic cost, to attitudes that have been exercised with approval during their formative years." The greatest single advantage of the abolition of censorship, it seems to me, would
be to make our culture more continuous, helping to free
child and adult from fear, inhibition, and guilt.

[The open distribution of pornography and obscenity
would thus encourage heterosexuality, and discourage impotence and frigidity. As such, it is life-giving, a stimulus to
joy and a source of socially harmless pleasure.] Despite the
forces of censorship, sexual intercourse is not a depraved and
shameful vice. It is a normal body function, habitual to the
judge's parents, George Washington, and many leaders of
the Girl Scouts. It will become habitual to our innocent
daughters, or we should hope that it will.

The true defense of pornography and obscenity, as they
encourage sexuality, is that they are harmless or beneficial. I
agree with the bawd in *Memoirs,* who "considered pleasure,
of one sort or another, as the universal port of destination,
and every wind that blew thither a good one, provided it
blew nobody any harm." In regard to censorship, the argument from literary merit is absurd and irrelevant. Of course
no work of serious literature should ever be banned, but Anthony Lewis, in his article "Sex—and the Supreme Court"
in *Esquire,* June 1963, is probably right in saying that after
the Supreme Court's Roth decision "no serious literary work
can now be termed constitutionally obscene."

Despite such temporary setbacks as the recent ruling by
the New York State Court of Appeals that *Tropic of Cancer*
is obscene, that battle appears to be won. It is the works
"without the slightest redeeming social importance" that
must be freed from censorship, or, rather, that [sexual stimu-

lation by symbol and image be recognized, in our time of bad marriages and worse non-marriages, as having redeeming social importance. I am aware that, the conditions of legislative reelection being what they are, obscenity laws are effectively unalterable at present. Then, judicial appointment being what *it* is, let them not be enforced.

As for the fact that so much pornography and obscenity is dreadful, that the *Memoirs* and the *Handbook* are not the worst of it but more nearly the best of it, that is a problem for literary criticism, not for jurisprudence. Leave them to the strangler's hands of the critic. It is his responsibility to say that Rechy's *City of Night* is illiterate trash, or Burroughs' *Naked Lunch* sadistic slop. But let them be published, and let those who want them buy them and read them. Experience and taste will save us, those of us who want to be saved.

Paul Goodman

Pornography, Art, and Censorship

PRESENT THINKING ABOUT OBSCENITY AND PORNOGRAPHY IS wrong-headed and damaging. In order to protect vital liberties, the higher, more intellectual courts often stand out against the police, the postmasters, and popular prejudice; yet since they don't give the right reasons, the issues are never settled. And worse, the courts lend themselves to the sexual attitude which, at this moment in our history, creates the very "hard-core" pornography that is objected to. That is, the court corrupts, it helps the censors corrupt. It ought to give light and provide leadership, and instead it stands in the way of progress. And worst of all, finally, by misunderstanding the nature of art and speech, the court emasculates them and prevents them from playing their indispensable social role. These are harsh words. Many of the readers of this magazine are going to be offended by this essay: they won't like my statement of the problem and they will think my remedies are worse than the disease. Nevertheless let us reason about it.

We are faced with the dilemmas of a society in transition. In discussing censorship, it is impossible to make good sense and good law without sociological psychological analysis; rehashing the statutes will not do. But it is no secret that in this field earnest authorities angrily clash on the most material issues (this is a sign of transition). Take the most undoubted sadistic pornography, socially worthless and sold at a criminal profit: one psychologist will say that its effects are disastrous, it causes "sex crimes" and juvenile delinquency; yet another psychologist will flatly assert that no such connection has ever been proved, there is no clear and present danger to warrant legal action. Now in this particular difficulty, the courts seem to have a convenient out: since admittedly the dubious object has no social merit, since its associations are unsavory and the purveyor is a racketeer, why shouldn't the court go along with the censorship? No real freedom is impugned. But here is a dilemma: *what if the censorship itself, part of a general repressive antisexuality, causes the evil, creates the need for sadistic pornography sold at a criminal profit?* The tone of the censorship—*and* of the usual court decisions—is vindictive and anxious; it is not the tone of a simple prudential choice in terms of broad social policy. The censoring is a dynamic and emotional act, with novel and perhaps unthought-of effects. The social question is not the freedom of a venal purveyor, though the case is always argued in his terms since he is the one brought to court; the question is whether the sexual climate of the community is being perverted by the censorship.

The censorship justifies itself as protection of children and adolescents. But consider this issue in terms of an accepted commonplace of contemporary pedagogy, that we must provide the child a "structured permissiveness" to grow in: permissiveness so that he can act without fear, shame, and resentment, and learn by his mistakes; and a structure of firm *parental* morals and culture, how "we" behave, with which he can identify when he needs security and guidance in his anxiety and confusion. A good parent rarely sees a clear and present danger (of the sort of being hit by a car or swallowing poison). Most dubious associations and behaviors of a child outgrow themselves in his ongoing career in a moral and cultural environment. And indeed, this ongoing career is the only real solution for him; whereas a "protective" parental attitude will almost surely communicate the parents' anxieties and complicate things further.

If this is a correct analysis, then the recent "liberal" decision on *Lady Chatterley's Lover* is inadequate. It is not permissive in the right way and it does not provide a firm moral and cultural support. I am urging the court to re-examine its own anxieties and ask if the pornographic is in fact, in our times, obscene.

I

Judge Bryan's exoneration of *Lady Chatterley* takes its doctrine from Woolsey on *Ulysses* (1933) and Brennan in *Roth v. United States* (1957). Let us consider these in turn.

Judge Woolsey's method in clearing *Ulysses* is as follows: he defines the obscene as the pornographic, as "tending to stir the sex impulses or to lead to sexually impure and lustful thoughts," and he proceeds to show that the book does neither but "is a sincere and serious attempt to devise a new literary method for the observation and description of mankind." Let us postpone the literary criticism till the next section, but here stop short at the definition of obscenity.

The notion that sexual impulse or stirring sexual impulse is a bad thing comes from an emotional climate in which it was generally agreed that it would be better if sexuality did not overtly exist, when people bathed and slept fully clothed, and a bull was called a he-cow. Then anything which was sexual in public, as by publication of "detailed representation in words or pictures," violated society's self-image and was certainly obscene. In our times such a notion cannot define obscenity. The pornographic is not *ipso facto* the obscene. As Judge Jerome Frank pointed out in 1949, "No sane man thinks that the arousing of normal sexual desires is socially dangerous." We live in a culture where all High Thought insists on the beauty and indeed hygienic indispensability of sexual desires, and where a vast part of commerce is busy in their stimulation. Nevertheless, Judge Bryan on *Chatterley* repeats the doctrine in 1960! This leaves us in utter confusion. For consider: Bryan goes on to define the "prurient . . . that is to say, shameful or morbid interest in sex"; but, if the stirring of desire is defined, and therefore treated, as obscene, how can a normal person's interest in sex be anything else *but* shameful? This is what shame is, the blush at finding one's impulse to be unacceptable. Only a brazen person would not be ashamed. So the court corrupts. It is a miserable social policy. I would rather have Lawrence condemned than defended by such reasoning.

But it is Woolsey's second clause, "leading to lustful thoughts," that is the more interesting, for this is the likely and immediate effect of literary or pictorial stimulation. Bluntly, "lustful thoughts" means incitement to masturbate; and I guess that in the overwhelming majority of cases this is the chief use of pornography. Let us again look to history. In the nineteenth century, all sexual facts were suspect, but masturbation was a mortal sin and the prelude to insanity. Let me quote from a great, good-humored, and liberal man, the prince of the Enlightenment: "Nothing weakens the mind as well as the body so much as the kind of lust directed toward oneself. It is entirely at variance with the nature of man. We must place it before the youth in all its horribleness," etc., etc. (Immanuel Kant, *On Education*). Contrast with this a philosopher of our own day: "Left to itself, infantile masturbation has, apparently, no bad effect upon health and no discoverable bad effect upon character; the bad effects which have been observed in both respects are, it seems, wholly attributable to attempts to stop it" (Bertrand Russell, *Education and the Good Life*). But this is pretty nearly the identical opinion of Benjamin Spock, M.D., in his pocket book of *Child Care* which is, I suppose, in every middle-class home in America (more than 12,000,000 copies of the paperback have been sold). And since the connection between pornography and juvenile delinquency is much touted, let me quote the identical opinion of a revered criminologist: "Masturbation is a habit without deleterious effects in itself, yet a source of behavior difficulties because of strong social disapproval" (Donald Taft).*

My point is not that the habit is good; it is morally otiose. But when the court says that stirring to masturbate is obscene, certainly the court corrupts. It is claimed that the court must judge according to public sentiment; but there is plenty of better public sentiment. Why must the police and the courts follow the worst part of the population instead of leading with the best? A more enlightened court would not solve these problems any more than it has created integration in the South; but, by the same example, a good decision is not irrelevant.

This brings us to the doctrine of *Roth v. United States*. The standards to be applied in determining obscenity, Bryan quotes Judge Brennan, are "whether to the average person, applying contemporary standards, the dominant theme of the material taken as a whole appeals to prurient interest." Part of this sentence, "the dominant theme taken as a

---

* Let me spell out the damage. According to sexologists the dangers in this act come from (a) inhibited performance, (b) guilt and shame of the act, (c) guilt about accompanying images. Our public policy obviously enhances the first two conditions, but it is also importantly responsible for the guilt-inducing images, for it associates lust with punishment and degradation and so creates sado-masochistic thoughts.

whole," is used by Bryan to prove that *Lady Chatterley* is a "serious" work, following the tactics of Woolsey, and again let us defer the literary criticism. Here let us stop at "applying contemporary standards," which is an attempt on the part of the court to cope with the changes in emotional climate that we have just been discussing. As Judge Bryan puts it, "Much of what is now accepted would have shocked the community to the core a generation ago." I don't think that this is a sufficient account. What is the history?

As one reviews the many cases in James Kilpatrick's *The Smut Peddlers* * (which, despite its outrageous title and a vulgar first chapter, has many good pages), one is struck by how, year after year, this theme of changing standards recurs in the decisions: "What was regarded as indecent in the days of the Floradora Sextette, is decent in the days of the fan dance." But what is most striking is that in the long chain of decisions over two generations, the standard becomes increasingly broader, in almost every respect: the bathing suits more scanty, the four-letter words more tolerable, the descriptions of the sexual act more realistic, the "unnatural" themes more mentionable. It is just this tendency through time that the courts fail to take into account as they judge each case. Therefore they are always behind, they miss the essential nature of the phenomena they are judging, and this has consequences.

The fact is that our generations are living through a general breakdown of repressive defenses, increasingly accelerating; and therefore a deepening social neurosis. Freud's doctrine, let us remember, is that it is not repression (total amnesia) that causes neurosis, but the failure of repression, so that repressed contents return in distorted guise. The process is irreversible; our culture has experienced too much of it to ban it, or frighten it, out of mind. Therefore the only recourse is to try to get, as methodically and safely as possible, to the end of it, so that the drives can reappear as them-

* Doubleday, 312 pp., $3.95.

selves and come to their own equilibrium. This involves undoing the repressive attitude itself. It is just in this that our high courts, like the Lords in England, could be excellent social counselors. With expert advisors they could try to forecast, and guide toward, a sane sexual policy. Instead, they cling to an outmoded concept of obscenity and they prevent outmoded statutes from becoming dead letters. At the same time, they are forced to cede to changing public taste and relax standards. Now this must lead to social chaos, as we are witnessing with the pornography, for so long as the attempted repressing continues, the repressed contents must continually emerge in more and more distorted form. And of course we also get legal chaos, as the court twists and turns to avoid the outmoded statutes.

For a writer like myself, there is a bitter irony in Bryan's statement that the previously shocking is now acceptable. Yes it is—because Flaubert, Ibsen, and Wedekind, and Dreiser, O'Neill, and Joyce paid their pound of flesh to the censor. They opened the ever new sensibility and were punished for it. Probably this is inevitable, and any advance worth having is worth suffering for; but it is a bitter proceeding. And now *Lady Chatterley* is accepted as a "community" art work just when it has ceased to be a living art work. Lawrence has explicitly told us that he wrote it "in defiance of convention"; that defiance, and its awkward rusticity, were its life. Now we are left merely with a rather neurotic fantasy of a frigid woman and a class-resentful "dominating" man. The court's lagging acceptance of bygone classics for the wrong reasons makes it difficult for a living classic to be accepted and exert an influence in the living community.

In the breakdown of repression, the artists do their part by first dreaming the forbidden thoughts, assuming the forbidden stances, and struggling to make sense. They cannot do otherwise, for they bring the social conflicts in their souls to public expression. But the court does not do its duty; and the critics (I will mention no names) go along with the court's convenience and lie and lie.

What is the court's duty as I see it? To set aside the definition of pornography as obscentiy—just as it set aside the doctrine of equal but separate facilities—and to clarify and further the best tendency of the sexual revolution. To call *not* obscene whatever tends to joy, love, and liveliness, including the stirring of lustful impulses and thoughts. I shall argue at the end of this paper that such a policy would tend to diminish pornography—make it not a big deal.

As it is, for well-known historical reasons, we live in a stimulating, unsatisfying society midway in transition; and while the liberal court hedges in embarrassment and the critics lie, the police and the administrators lurk to get convictions on any grounds. The police make wholesale raids for girlie magazines, they entrap a harmless old man for his lustful habit, the postmaster bars Lawrence from the mails, and the Drug Administrator burns the books of Wilhelm Reich as "labels" for a contraband commodity. To restore order, there has to be a wiser policy.

II

Let me proceed to a philosophical question raised by these decisions, which is, in my opinion, even more important for our society than the sexual matter: what is the nature of speech and art? To protect their "serious" books, the courts attempt to distinguish speech as communication of an idea or even as talking *about* a subject, from speech as an action doing something to its speaker, subject, and hearer. This is the tactic of Woolsey when he devotes most of his opinion to Joyce's "new method for the observation and description of mankind" and of Bryan when he says that the plot of *Lady Chatterley's Lover* "serves as a vehicle through which Lawrence develops his basic . . . philosophy. Most of the characters are prototypes." The judges reason that if something like this can be established, a book can be protected under the Bill of Rights guarantee of freedom to communicate opinion. Yet, although this is a useful distinction for some kinds of speech—e.g. scientific reporting and conscientious journalism—it simply does not apply to common speech, and it is necessarily irrelevant to art, for one essential function of art is to move the audience. If Joyce and Lawrence felt that all they had done was to convey ideas, they would have considered themselves failures.

(Naturally the decisions themselves, based on an unphilosophical distinction, have been notoriously inconsistent. For example, *The Well of Loneliness* was banned because "it seeks to justify the right of a pervert . . . it does not argue for repression of insidious impulses . . . it seeks to justify and idealize perverted ideas." Yet these are merely the ideas of the author. But contrariwise, Justice Stewart defended the film of *Lady Chatterley* by saying, "The picture advocates an idea—that adultery under certain circumstances may be proper behavior. The First Amendment guarantee is freedom to advocate ideas." Jerome Frank has wryly commented that if an "idea" is eloquently argued, it is in danger; if it is dully argued, it is safe.)

Here is an example of the legal doctrine at work. At the Marble Arch in London, crowds gather to listen to popular orators vent their grievances and longings on every topic under the sun, freedom for Nigeria, a subscription for the Irish Revolutionary Army, the ethics of deceiving one's wife, the nearest way to salvation. Like Bernard Shaw, the orators test their repartee against a powerfully insolent audience. All is strictly legal. But if a man comes within twenty-four inches of the speaker, he is at once hauled off by a guardian bobby! A man can say anything, but he mustn't do anything; he can listen to anything, but he mustn't let himself be aroused. Freedom of speech means freedom to talk about. Speech is not saying-as-an-action. The limitations are clear. If there would be incitement to riot, the freedom would cease. "Fighting words" are forbidden because they lead to fights. Pornography is forbidden because it is in the nature of detailed sexual reporting that it leads to physiological reactions and likely acts. Blasphemy and obscenity are forbidden because they are acts as such, they break a taboo in their very utterance, as well as presumably undamming what is held in repression by the taboo. Also, there are even particular topics, like the subject of *Lolita,* where merely to treat them at all in some public way is tantamount to sanctioning their existence in the universe. Here speech becomes magic, to name the Name creates the thing.

Jefferson and other revolutionaries who insisted on the Bill of Rights probably had a more risky notion of freedom of speech than our courts, as they did of political action in general. But if to them freedom of speech meant merely freedom to communicate opinions, they could not have intended the First Amendment to apply to belles-lettres at all, for the neoclassical aesthetic doctrine of their time held that the function of art was to move and instruct, to instruct by moving. In our modern aesthetics the legal embarrassment is even worse; we pay less attention to imitating reality and lay all the more emphasis on speech as action. To Freud, the art-act alleviates a repressed conflict by daring to express and publish it (this is Lawrence's "defying convention"). In advance-guard art, where the artist is reacting to and vomiting up something intolerable in society, the art-act cannot help being offensive. Since the nineteenth century, the naturalists have meant to defy and shame when they stripped away the mask of hypocrisy. The primary aim of Dada is to shock. In his *Theater of Violence,* Antonin Artaud declares that theater is precisely not communicating ideas but acting on the community, and he praises the Balinese village dance that works on dancers and audience till they fall down in a trance. (For that matter, the shrieking and wailing that was the specialty of Greek tragedy would among us cause a breach of the peace. The nearest we come are adolescent jazz sessions that create a public nuisance.) The "poetry readings" of the Beats try to give us their "existent situation," usually drunken, and the audience copes with it as best it can. I could continue a long list.

To these facts of modern art, the doctrine of Woolsey, Brennan, and van Pelt Bryan is not adequate. Such art cannot be defended as communicating ideas, and anything objectionable in it (there is much) must condemn it. Indeed, the arguments of the censoring customs officer or postmaster betoken a more genuine art-response, for they have been directly moved, although in an ignorant way, by the excitement and inner conflict of Joyce and Lawrence. Their experience is ignorant and low-grade because they are unwilling to let the sexual excitement belong to a larger world, and this is why they excerpt passages. But at least they have been made to feel that the world is threateningly sexual. As the British Magistrate Mead said, on paintings by Lawrence, "Art is immaterial. . . . Obscene pictures should be put an end to like any wild animal which may be dangerous." And so Justice Manton, in his dissent on *Ulysses,* "Obscenity is not rendered less by the statement of truthful fact," for it is precisely the fact, the nature of things, that is obscene to the censor.

Woolsey's doctrine is insulting to the artist. He says that the book did "not tend to excite lustful thoughts, *but* the net effect was a tragic and powerful commentary" (italics mine). Surely the author wants to say, "It is lustful among other things, and *therefore* its net effect is tragic."

In our culture an artist is expected to move the reader; he is supposed to move him to tears, to laughter, to indignation, to compassion, even to hatred; but he may not move him to have an erection or to mockery of public figures making a spectacle of themselves. Why not? By these restrictions we doom ourselves to a passionless and conformist community. Instead of bracketing off the "classics," as especially the British courts do—indeed, the legal definition of a classic seems to be a "non-actionable obscenity"—let us pay attention to the classical pornography and we shall see that it is not the case, as the court feels obliged to prove, that a work has a "net" social use despite its sexual effect, but rather that the pornography, in a great context and spoken by a great soul, *is* the social use. Aristophanic comedy was still close to a seasonal ritual to encourage rebelliousness and lead to procreation. Rabelais is disgraceful like a giant baby, and this *is* the Renaissance. Catullus teaches us the callous innocence of highborn youth, free of timidity and pettiness; and Tom Jones is a similar type, with a dash of English sentimentality. If we may believe their preludes, both the *Arabian Nights* and the *Decameron* are cries of life in the face of death; and in our times Jean Genet, one of our few fine writers, is pornographic and psychopathic because only so, he tells us, can he feel that he exists in our inhuman world. But apart from these lofty uses, there are also famous pornographic books made just for fun, since sex is a jolly subject.

To explore the nature of speech as action, consider the other forbidden topic, the mockery of sacred public figures. In our country we suffer from a gentleman's agreement that is politically and artistically disastrous. For instance, our recent President could not frame an English sentence, and according to some observers his career as the head of a great university was dismally hilarious. "Dwight Eisenhower at Columbia" is a title to rouse an Aristophanes. In the eighteenth century Ike would have been richly mauled. But our satirists on stage and TV avoid such subjects. Then there cannot be great comedy, for if you dare not mock the pink elephant looming in the foreground, you can't mock anything. Instead, our satire consists of isolated gags that do not add up to an explosion. But satire is an essential of democracy, for how can we expect our leaders to be anything but front-figures if they do not take any personal risk and cannot be stung?

The court is not philosophical. It does not see that lively speech is active speech. Sexual action is a proper action of art. The question is not *whether* pornography, but the quality of the pornography. To sting powerful figures into a personal engagement is a proper action of art, otherwise we sink in a faceless swamp. What the more intellectual court does do is to protect exceptional cases against vulgar prejudices and police busy-work. (But often, as in the astounding case of the revocation of Bertrand Russell's appointment at New York's City College, the matter never gets to a better court.) This is not enough to improve the cultural climate. In principle, the living writers are not exceptional and famous cases. Rather, it works out as follows: publishers will not publish what will get them into trouble; authors cease to write what will not be published, or what the editor censors the heart out of; soon the public has lost its authors at their best, and the authors have lost the common touch. The actual situation is that there is little that is published, and perhaps not much that is written, that does or would get into trouble with the censorship, except precisely the hard-core pornography. Why is there so little? If the publishers and authors were doing their duty, the courts would be battlegrounds. Instead, the void is soon filled with safe entertainers, gag-men, sensation-mongers, pap-journalists. Advertising is the chief public art. The community is starved of ideas.

III

It has become the fashion to say that the aesthetic and libertarian matters we have been discussing have no relation to the actual police problem of hard-core pornography; let the police be careful not to encroach on serious writers, and let the writers leave the police to their raids and entrapment. This schizophrenic theory is false. We are one community, and the kind of high culture we have and the kind of low culture we have are opposite faces of the same lead quarter. But let us look at the hard-core pornography in itself: *

---

* Most simply, we must bear in mind the remark of William Sloane of Rutgers, cited by James Kilpatrick: "I am unimpressed with the record of repressive legislation in this country. The laws against narcotics, for example, are

I have been arguing in this essay that not only is there innocent and useful pornography that ought not to be censored, but the method of censorship helps create the very kind of harmful pornography that we should like to see checked. The case is similiar—and not causally unrelated —to the social creation of juvenile delinquency by social efforts to control it. When excellent human power is inhibited and condemned, it will reappear ugly and dangerous. The censorious attitude toward the magazines and pictures is part of the general censorious attitude that hampers ordinary sexuality and thereby heightens the need for satisfaction by means of the magazines and pictures. It is said that the pornography artificially stimulates, and no doubt this is true (though there is no evidence that there can be such a thing as "too much" sex), but it is not so importantly true as that the pornography is indulged in because of a prior imbalance of excessive stimulation and inadequate discharge. Given such an imbalance, if the pornography heightens satisfaction, as it probably does in many cases, it is insofar therapeutic. This is an unpleasant picture of our country, but there is no help for it except to remedy antisexuality. I have argued that the revolution is irreversible, and the attempt to re-establish total amnesia must lead to more virulent expressions, e.g. still less desirable pornography.

Let us consider two aspects of poor pornography, its *mere* sexuality or "lust," devoid of any further human contact, drama, or meaning; and its very frequent sado-masochism.

The experience of mere "lust" in isolation is a neurotic artifact. Normally, affection increases lust and pleasure leads to

supporting a large criminal class and leading to large-scale corruption of our youth. The laws against off-track betting are supporting a large criminal class and lead directly to police corruption. No set of laws will prevent the bootlegging of pornography." But they *will* make it profitable. When J. Edgar Hoover favors us with his periodic philippics about the frighteningly increasing rate of crime, flood of pornography, theft of autos, etc., and asks for more teeth in the laws and more money for enforcement, surely he proves too much. There is the possibility that his methods, since they do not work, might be the wrong methods.

gratitude and affection. The type neurotic case is the sailor ashore, who seeks out a "pig" and works very hard *not* to get emotionally involved. Why should he behave so strangely? Let me suggest an explanation. His promiscuity is approved by his peers but, more deeply and morally, it is disapproved by himself. If he regarded the woman as a person, he would feel guilty and hate her, and sometimes he manifests this as brutal violence, really meant for himself. More decently he restricts his experience to bare lust, though this is not much of a *sexual* experience. I choose the example because it is a fair analogy of the attitude of a large population in America, not unknown in middle-class suburbs. We accept the natural-ness of sexuality in an abstract and permissive way, but we have by no means come to terms with its moral, family, and pedagogic dilemmas during a hard period of transition. There then occurs an isolated "sexuality" which at its best is hy-gienic and at its worst is mate-swapping, disowning the sex-uality of those we love. Finally, I would suggest that this is the style of much of what the court elegantly calls "dirt for dirt's sake," the sexually stimulating without dramatic, plas-tic, or other artistic value. Necessarily this must be limited to a few stereotyped anecdotes and a few naked poses; and it must soon become boring.

The sado-masochistic pornography, however, that com-bines lust and punishment, torture, or humiliation, is the darker effect of a more restrictive and guilty-making train-ing, for example certain kinds of religious upbringing. There are comparatively few real-life sado-masochists, but all the more do the smash hits of popular culture cultivate fan-tasies that proceed in guilt and end in punishment, genre of Tennessee Williams. This calamitous requirement, that the lust be punished, used to be a standard of legality employed by learned judges. How stupid can grown men be! For the consumer, such fantasies have a dual advantage: they satisfy both the need for righteousness (sadistic superego) and the "weakness" of giving in to pleasure; they embody an exciting conflict. But the bother with such images when used pri-vately as pornography is that they are socially disapproved and enhance individual guilt; the excitement proceeds against strong resistance, and mounting fear, and often dies; and there is a tendency to raise the ante. It is said that this kind of pornography creates juvenile delinquents; my hunch is rather that the type of delinquent who has a need to prove his potency has a hankering for such pornography, all the better if it can be combined with cerebral know-how, as in hipster literature. Nevertheless, it doesn't do him any good, for, on balance, it increases tension.

From even such rudimentary analysis, it is clear that we can differentiate the moral quality of various pornography and make a rough rating of useful, indifferent, damaging. The social question, obviously, is how to improve the first and eliminate the last. Police courts and administrative officers, however, and even jury courts and high courts, are hardly the right forum for important and subtle moral debates. But expert opinion doesn't agree either; I could quote a crashing dissent to every proposition I have been making (except this one). Still, I am even less impressed by the bellow of J. Edgar Hoover that the police cannot wait for the experts to make up their minds, since one of the few things that is demonstrable is that ignorant suppression is wrong.

   Yet I do not think that moral problems are private problems and can be left alone. Here I must dissent from my bold and honest classmate Judge Murtagh, who wants to leave most such issues to a person's conscience before God. On the contrary, it is because moral problems are so publicly important that they must be ongoingly decided by the whole public; and they are so subtle that only the manifold mind of all the institutions of society, skirmishing and experimenting, can figure them out and invent right solutions. In this essay I have been proposing to the judges a particular public experiment, a particular "firm morals and culture" and "permissiveness" in which there might be both the ongoing solution of these social evil and, more important, a growth into a more living culture. Let us speculate about it. Suppose that the courts altered their previous doctrine, as I have suggested, and now decided that it was not obscene to stir sexual desires and thoughts. And suppose that at the same time they somehow strengthened the requirement of a provable social or human utility (as would be a reasonable requirement for TV stations, for instance, since they use the public channels). This decision would simply express our best present-day thinking: that sexual feeling is a *fine* part of life and it is a *part* of life.

What might occur?

An immediate effect of this drastic change would be to open to the legal public media a very large, and I think soon preponderant, part of the traffic that is now subterranean and culturally uncontrolled. This is an advantage, for now the traffic can meet open evaluation, the appraisal of critics, the storm of angry letters that frightens advertisers.

In principle anything might now be shown, from a hint of sexual desire to the drama of the sexual act itself. Since the change-over would be so drastic, the court might aim at a deliberate slowness, and the great mass media would wisely want to meet together and agree on a prudent rate of change. The test of proper deliberateness would be that, *regarded as mere isolated and excerpted pornography*, showing the act would be little more interesting than the hint. And in between, it is hoped, there would develop the habit of treating sexual facts as the common part of life which they are.

Artistically, of course, the extremes are quite different, for it requires a setting of powerful passion and beauty to make artistically workable so vivid a scene as the sexual act. And indeed, one of the most salutary and hoped-for effects of the change I am proposing would be the radical diminution in sheer quantity, and the improvement in variety and quality, of the hundreds of shows that a person exposes himself to every year. Since at present the stimulation is low-grade, the repetition is chronic; perhaps if the experience were fuller, there would be less repetition. Perhaps we could have something else than the endless westerns, crime stories, and romances if there were more animal satisfaction and not merely the stereotyped symbolic satisfactions that these genres offer, with the sex climaxing in shooting, which for some reason can be shown. As it is, the public never gets beyond sex and violence. *Culturally, the greatest curse of censorship is that it produces too many and too trivial art works, all of them inhibitedly pornographic.*

The aim is to establish a principled general policy. The states and localities could continue to enforce whatever censorship they please, so long as they do not risk a national suit and are content to do without some of the national culture. The situation, as I envisage it, is somewhat the opposite of the school-integration decision; for the federal court is not intervening in any region, but is insisting that national policy must provide intellectual and historical leadership unhampered by local prejudices; yet as far as possible it will keep hands off to allow for various regional experimentation. This is not the effect of the court's present policy— e.g. in opening *Lady Chatterley* to the mails—for that does do violence to local sensibilities, necessarily, in order to give some scope for mature experience. But if these were a more principled general policy, and the courts were not continually obliged to fight, a generation too late, a rear-guard action against morons, the nation could allow the localities to be much *more* restrictive and self-defensive; in order to protect local option, they could even uphold the postmaster. It is possible in a federal system to decentralize the cultural climate. This allows for experiment and for citizens to have a freer choice of the life that suits their needs; but there must be freedom to experiment. Now we have the worst of the contrary situation: a degenerate centralism, a conformist mass made of the lowest common denominator of the narrow provincial multiplied by the venality of Hollywood and Madison Avenue.

Legalized pornography would, naturally, deplete the criminal market. (As Morris Ernst has speculated, the price on dirty postcards would drop from three for a dollar to three for a nickel.) In my cynical opinion, a first effect would be that the great publishers, networks, and film producers that now righteously keep their skirts clean and censor the prose and poetry of their moral and intellectual betters would eagerly cash in. But a fairly quick effect, it is to be hoped, would be that such isolated pornography as a genre would simply become boring and diminish, just as women's short skirts today create not a flurry.

Finally, there would be immense cultural advantages. Less embarrassment, a franker language, and a more sensual feeling would magnify and ennoble all our art and perhaps bring some life to the popular culture; and conversely, the exposure to such art would help to humanize sexuality and break down the neurotic compartment of "mere lust." In the difficulties of our modern sexual transition—where we do not know the best form of the family, the proper attitude toward premarital and extramarital sex, nor even what physical behavior is "normal"—we certainly can profit from the warm fantasy of these subjects in lyric and tragic art. And not least, any social change in the direction of permissiveness and practical approval, which integrates sexual expression with other ordinary or esteemed activities of life, must diminish the need to combine sex with punishment and degradation. To increase the possibility of satisfaction in real situations is to make unnecessary the hipster struggle for violent and apocalyptic experiences.

My argument is a simple one: a more principled high-level policy on obscenity, which realistically takes into account the tendency of our mores, would facilitate the moral and cultural structuring that can alone solve the problems of hard-core pornography; and it would also have beautiful cultural advantages. Whereas the present attempted repression by the police, administrators, and lower courts not only must continue to fail but keeps creating the evil it combats. Certainly many earnest people would consider the remedy I suggest to be worse than the disease, and they would prefer to muddle along. I am not sure that we can.

Peter Michelson

An Apology for Pornography

TRICKSTER, THE ARCHETYPAL FOOL OF WINNEBAGO INDIAN mythology, was possessed of a phallus so large that he had to carry it over his shoulder. He did not, according to the legend, know either what it was or how it was to be used. But its very bulk reassured him against those who ridiculed his subjection to the huge burden and claimed he could not rid himself of it. For to carry it required, after all, a substantial and unique strength. This mockery, however, eventually took its toll, and Trickster wearied of the weight and mystery; he determined therefore to remove them. Whereupon he discovered, of course, that the joke was on him. Great as it was, his strength could not equably bear the burden, nor his wit devise a release from it.

This is a sobering myth. Rather than celebrating power and potency, like most phallic legends, it documents man's sexual anxiety and ignorance. But it is honest, more honest than men customarily are about their sexuality. There are, for instance, primitive Australian tribes whose traditional teaching does not recognize that copulation causes pregnancy. And the traditions are honored; pregnancy is explained by the woman having slept under a certain tree or having been graced by the light of the moon. In their hearts—and presumably their loins—they may know what's what, but they must speak with a forked tongue.

Nor is this paralyzing duality peculiar to primitive cultures. The stable civilized culture is even more afraid of its own beastly libido (this neurosis is the subject of Wayland Young's *Eros Denied*). Whether rational (as in Plato's *Republic*) or hysterical (as in the Salem witch trials), such a fear attacks the culture's particular libido image. The literature of sexuality has been every bit as victimized by hysteria as were Sacco and Vanzetti. Pornography, it is supposed, constitutes both a social and psychic threat. Society will be terrorized by the rampant lewdness induced by pornographic books—our wives and daughters raped, law and order dissolved. And our sons (somebody has to do the raping) will either be driven to mad carnality or will become idiots driveling in the wake of luxurious onanism. *We*—*i.e.* the patriarchal we—of course remain impervious.

The legal starting point is the social threat. And here the machinations of the courts at all levels to find evidence of social value in "pornographic" books have resulted in monumental irrelevance. While there are responsible decisions, such as Judge Woolsey's judgment in favor of *Ulysses*, their irony is that, however good they are in particular, they are based on the wrongheaded obscenity laws. Judge Woolsey was critically right to find that *Ulysses* is a complex work, the end of which is not obscenity. But he felt compelled to explain away the pornography and obscenity that are in the novel in order to grant its freedom. The real issue is articulated by Judge Frank's dissenting opinion about the Roth case in 1956. He defined the issue as whether or not pornography, quite distinctly from its social or artistic merit, constitutes a "clear and present danger" to society. He argues that there is no evidence that it does and that such research as has been done is either inconclusive or negates the idea that crimes or neuroses are caused by pornography. Until such time as there is evidence of this, Judge Frank's seems to me the only reasonable standard. There is nevertheless the kind of decision reached through the Supreme Court's recent caprice in the Ginzburg case. In that decision, incisively criticized by Justice Douglas, the character of the book is determined by the kind of advertising with which it is merchandised! An observation of censorship in *Rights and Writers* suggests the sort of patriarchal hysteria which seems to prompt such decisions: "We know of no case where any juror or judge has admitted that *he* found material erotically stimulating or a stimulus to irregular conduct; on the contrary, the expression of concern is always that someone else or some other class of people will be corrupted."

We don't prosecute books or television for misrepresenting marriage, or politics, or religion, or war. But we do prosecute where we think sex has been misrepresented. Plato, for all the dangers of his moral metaphysics, would have at least prosecuted all supposed stupidities equally. It would be neither more nor less criminal in his republic to represent man as pure sexuality than it would be to represent marriage as pure idyll or God as pure saccharine.

As usual in the event of emergency, it's women and children first. But such data as we have (e.g. the Kinsey reports, and the Glueck studies for the Harvard Law School) indicate that pornography has little or no effect on women or children. There probably is a psychic threat, but a threat no greater than that posed by any popular fantasy literature.

Emma Bovary shows that a mind deluded by romance will make a bad job of reality. That is the danger of romance or fantasy whenever and in whatever way it dominates the mind. And pornography is a kind of romance but no more socially or psychically pernicious than the romance of passion that dominates the lives of Emma Bovary or Heathcliff or the mundane romance of *Please Don't Eat the Daisies*. The representation of life as all passion or all idyll or all sexuality is a delusion but not one that will determine the behavior of any but an already pathological personality. A *preoccupation* with pornography or any other kind of romance may be an index of mental imbalance or even potential criminality, but it is certainly not a cause.

LIMITLESS POTENCY, LIMITLESS LIBIDO

To understand the contemporary working of pornography we must conceive the term in its widest context. Originally it signified writings about prostitutes. But as amateur promiscuity has increasingly supplied erotic fantasy material, pornography has created a new and larger being, *homo sexualis*. This has two images, the erect phallus and the carnal woman. The phallic symbol has become not only a psychological and literary commonplace, but also a cultural joke, and we are long since accustomed to finding one in everything from a new Buick to the Empire State Building. But the female image of *homo sexualis*—the essential pornographic image—is never funny, even in parody. Al Capp's cartoon women, for example, parody this image, enormously breasted and buttocked. But even the parody rides the edge of lust, and these images are much more desirable than ridiculous. For the pornographic world is peopled with men of limitless potency and women of limitless libido. O, the protagonist in *Story of O,* is a good contemporary example. No concerns in the narrative are allowed to obscure the translation of her total existence into terms of sexuality.

In what is perhaps the best critical study of pornography, *Pornography and the Law,* Eberhard and Phyllis Kronhausen observe that "Both erotic realism and pornography, each in their own way, fulfill certain functions and answer basic needs in the human psyche which have been recognized by many societies and periods; for instance, in ancient Greece and Rome, in the Near East, as well as in China, Japan and India, where erotic art and literature have always been integral parts of the total culture." In whatever art form, pornography documents both man's neurotic and his archetypal concern with sexuality. The neurotic (not to be confused with the pathological) engagement with pornography is the private confrontation of the individual psyche with its sexual needs. The larger cultural engagement with pornography is the public confrontation with archetypal—and usually subliminal—sexual impulses. Pornography then, for better or worse, is the imaginative record of man's sexual will. Let's look briefly at some of the implications of this.

Steven Marcus (*The Other Victorians*) suggests that there is an inverse correspondence between a rising concentration on the dominating and sadistic image of masculine sexuality in pornography and the diminishing actuality of these qualities in real life. He finds evidence for this in the extravagant sense of phallic power so characteristic of pornography, where, as he puts it, "the penis becomes the man: it does the thrusting and not the man; it is its own agent." And in the world of pornography, where sexuality is the prime mover, the penis takes on a kind of omnipotence. Marcus tends to regard this extravagant phallic metaphor as another sign of pornography's juvenility. But its psychological dimensions signify something well beyond the rhetorical crudeness of its masculine vanity.

In her book *Psychic Energy* M. Esther Harding, a colleague and student of Jung, analyzes what might be called the sexual ages of man. The earliest stages are phallic, in which man is synecdochically conceived as penis. There are intermediate stages, where sexuality is stylized and idealized.

The graphic representations of the early stages are of course the graffiti of the ages—phallic imagery and symbology. The intermediate stages are represented in the expansion of man's image from penis alone to the whole body—e.g. in stylized nude statuary. The advanced stages, dealing in emotional as well as physical sexuality, are more difficult of representation. The dynamics of psychic sexuality are beyond the static restrictions of painting and sculpture, but perhaps the film can overcome this. Yukio Mishima's recent film *Rites of Love and Death* or the Swedish film *Dear John* may be examples. But the point is that we do experience these archetypal sexual ages, perhaps all of them simultaneously, and in both a personal and cultural context. And it is a natural impulse to express them. Pornography, in the sense that I am defining it, is the primal manner of this expression. As our knowledge of sexuality increases and is assimilated into the culture, as psychological studies (we are still explicating Freud, Jung, *et al.*), sociological studies (such as the Kinsey reports), and physiological studies (such as Masters' and Johnson's recent *Human Sexual Response*) give us greater understanding of human sexuality, so will pornography, the literature of that sexuality, exhibit a greater artistic sophistication.

A comparison of the contemporary *Story of O* with the eighteenth-century *Memoirs of a Woman of Pleasure (Fanny Hill)* will authenticate this evolutionary progress. *Fanny Hill* describes a prostitute's life, with the end of exploiting the obvious orgasmic stimuli in the subject. Fantasy is central to this end, and to induce it a kind of realism is affected through description of an occupation where rampant sexuality is made believable so that the reader can identify with it. Thus the action adopts the epistolary narrative device, the trappings of a specific sociological setting (eighteenth-century London), and is resolved with a gratuitous moral apostrophe on virtue and honor. In these respects it parodies the techniques of the eighteenth-century novel. Fanny's first letter puts it thus: "Truth! stark, naked truth, is the word; and

I will not so much as take the pains to bestow the strip of a gauze wrapper on it, but paint situations such as they actually rose to me in nature, careless of violating those laws of decency that were never made for such unreserved intimacies as ours; and you have too much sense, too much knowledge of the ORIGINALS themselves, to sniff prudishly and out of character at the PICTURES of them. The greatest men, those of the first and most leading taste, will not scruple adorning their private closets with nudities, though, in compliance with vulgar prejudices, they may not think them decent decorations of the staircase, or salon."

This is a good and true argument. But it is rather a rhetorical gambit persuading the reader to believe in the descriptions and not feel guilt, which would of course ruin their effect. From this point the novel turns a standard eighteenth-century plot into a paradise of erotic fantasy. Fanny, a poor, provincial innocent, goes to London where she is deflowered and debauched by urban decadence and aristocratic profligacy. In a nice touch, the story is resolved when Fanny is reunited with her first despoiler and true love; they marry and live ever after in virtue, honor and penitence. The key here is that the story is essentially description of sexual acts to the end of inducing some kind of orgasmic fantasy. Although the standard situations of the early English novel are employed—Fanny's world is shot through with the vicissitudes of poverty and innocence in the clutches of City and Aristocracy—the story is altogether focused on fantastic sexuality. There is a suggestion of moral causality, but it is so slight and so overshadowed by sex that it signifies nothing. There is no attempt to *explore* any of the implicit moral or psychic problems.

STORY OF O

The essence of *Fanny Hill* is simplicity, simplicity of theme and simplicity of description. *Story of O,* on the other hand, adopts the complexity of abstraction and metaphor so characteristic of the modern novel. It is a metaphor of love as libido. If that figure contains all the paraphernalia of pornography—whips, chains, tortures, sadism, masochism, masculine power, feminine submission, sexual anonymity (At one point O is blindfolded and brought into a room where "*A* hand seized one of her breasts, *a* mouth fastened on the tip of the other." Sex without superego.), and so on —it also contains the complex apparatus of the psyche. O submits herself to a brotherhood of sexuality which exploits and punishes her body, exorcises her will, dominates her total being, and finally is the cause of her self-destruction. She gives herself again to her surrogate lover, proving and taking refuge in her capacity of love; he abandons her also and she kills herself, but only after securing her master's permission.

The story provides, thus, two erotic points of view. From the masculine perspective it describes a complete liberation of the sexual libido. Men possess and enjoy O anonymously, without consequence or emotional responsibility. Her need for love brings her to them, which is a nice male power fantasy. And once they are through with her she is simply discarded; they have in fact the power of life and death, another nice male power fantasy. But from the female viewpoint the story arouses intense anxiety, a sure antidote to pornographic fantasy. O's captivity may be ended whenever she wishes, but to wish it is to forfeit the love she so desperately needs. Thus she is confronted constantly by the fear of loss. And of course she does lose that love, twice. And the consequence is suicide. Here is another classic female anxiety, that love for a man will subsume self-identity, and the loss of the love will leave her without reason to be.

What is important here is that O becomes the ur-woman in quest of love. She is thus exposed to its complete domination and consequent agony. Is she, then, an allegorical figure, perhaps the first *Everywoman?* Certainly everything about her is feminine stereotype—her love, her submissiveness, her sexuality, her annihilation of self, her anxieties, everything. At one point in *Peyton Place* (also written, remember, by a woman) a young girl says to her paramour, "Come on Honey. Love me a little. . . . Come on Honey. . . . Hard. . . . Do it hard, Honey. Bite me a little. Hurt me a little." This is O's position; except she says, "Hurt me a *lot*." On the one hand, she is the answer to every man's secret dream. On the other hand, she is an object awful in her implications. It is the former quality that makes her story pornographic. And it is the latter quality that takes her story beyond simplistic exploitation of sexual fantasy and lets it metaphorically explore a fundamental human condition.

Admittedly, these examples have higher artistic claims than most pornography. But I am interested here in its nature and artistic potential, and must consider therefore its highest stages of development. The hard core or commercial pornography is static and its ends are served by the simplest of descriptive techniques and rhetorical gambits (see Eberhard and Phyllis Kronhausen's *Pornography and the Law* and Steven Marcus' *The Other Victorians* for analyses of pornographic structure). But there is another and higher form of pornography which might be called *literary;* it is an exploration of human sexuality. This is real pornography (not what the Kronhausens call erotic realism). It does more than exploit its subject. We are, as Freud observed, *all* of us more or less neurotic. One aspect of human neurosis is the rhythm of expectations and frustrations which marks our sexual lives. Pornography on its lowest level exploits this rhythm by providing easy fantasy gratifications. On its highest level it *explores* this rhythm, its moral and psychic implications, and to the degree that it does this it is poetic. This is the pornography being absorbed into what we call Literature, and it is represented by such works as *O*. The fact of pornography's evolution out of its own genre and into the larger literature means that pornography must also be considered as a rhetorical device for that literature. Faulkner, for example, although no mere pornographer, is certainly one of the most pornographic of modern writers. He often uses por-

nographic scenes and situations (the cockpit copulation in
Pylon, the romance of Mink Snopes in *The Hamlet,* etc.) to
articulate his total scheme. It is perhaps in this latter rhetorical role that pornography will assume its final form and
have its greatest significance.

DENYING HUMAN SEXUALITY

What I have been arguing is that pornography, like any literature, is a way of knowing. The irony of its subject, sex, is
the irony of another social pariah, the whore. We either
deny its literary existence or privately acknowledge our private intimacies with it; and we are correspondingly either as-
tonished or embarrassed to meet it on the street. Critically,
if we don't ignore pornography altogether, we condescend to
it like reformed sugar-daddies. Legally we invoke "contemporary community standards" against it, as if they were not a
fantasy morality derived from vestigial Puritanism rather
than human experience. And thus we insure our ignorance
of what it can tell us about the interaction of moral imagination and sexual being. Meanwhile science, having escaped
community standards and academic condescension in the
guise of a white coat, goes on documenting a reality we deny
our imagination.

For Plato the true was necessarily the beautiful. For us the
true is much more likely to be the ugly or grotesque. A
whole tradition argues this. Stanley Kowalski calls on his
"colored lights," but it is finally the bright white light of
revelation that brings the play's moment of truth and
beauty—Blanche, Stanley, and Mitch all exposed, ugly,
and helpless. And Martha and George in *Who's Afraid of
Virginia Woolf* expend their full energies to show their
young guests the true, the blushful Hippocrene—their
monumental ugliness. Our literature adopts an aesthetic that
aims to reveal the ugly as the true, and it often uses the sexual libido, which our culture has turned into a species of the
ugly, as part of its rhetoric.

For the eighteenth and nineteenth centuries ugliness was artistically tolerable only when used as a dialectical agent (e.g. satire) to enforce the idea of a beautiful and harmonious nature. It was an aesthetic that dismissed all aberrations as irrelevant. Contemporary aesthetic practice uses this process but reverses the values. Like Satan, it says, "Evil, be thou my good," and plays the role of devil's advocate, using the ugly to penetrate a cosmos no longer thought to be either benevolent or harmonious. It is at best indifferent, at worst malign. The ugly, then, becomes an ironic figure of revelation, exposing an implacable universe unrelieved by moral or spiritual design. Sartre's concepts of *slime* and *nausea* are eloquent statements of an aesthetic of the ugly. And the Theater of the Absurd is its most prominent practitioner. Pornography, the kind represented by *Story of O,* is a manifestation of the ugly. It does not romanticize sexuality; sex, unlike John's other wife, is not beautiful. It is simply there, at the center of man's life, dominating love, aspiration, happiness, all human experience.

Perhaps, as Freud suggests, our sexual impulses cannot be gratified without being cultural outlaws. Perhaps sexuality requires being worked out through cultural taboos. If so, this argues a fearful human necessity. We take LSD trips in an effort to find (or escape from) the true and maybe the beautiful. The danger is that our vision (perhaps of ourselves) will be destructive and make us flip altogether. But our ignorance is desperate enough so that we take the risk. Although the dangers are much smaller, pornography is part of this contemporaneous urgency to pursue the true. It too explores the unknown and therefore fearful in us. Our glimpses into that world refute our private and public lies. We can keep going—into the psyche as into space—and risk the dislocations that new knowledge brings, or we can collapse at the naked sight of ourselves. Not to explore the impulse to pornography is a form of denying human sexuality. We are, willy-nilly, brought to the overriding question of the modern imagination: how much deceit can we afford?

George P. Elliott

Against Pornography

PORNOGRAPHY IS LIKE A SQUALID, UNNECESSARY LITTLE COUN-
try which owes its independence to a vagary of history. But,
though pornography is seldom of much importance, it may
be of considerable interest, for to talk about it is unavoida-
bly to talk about the Great Powers adjacent to it. Pornography speaks the language of Art; in recent centuries it has
come within the sphere of influence of the Law; Psychology
and Morals have vested interests in it. Moreover, occasionally pornography becomes genuinely important—when it
is used as a seat of operations by the erotic nihilists who

would like to destroy every sort of social and moral law and who devote their effective energies to subverting society as such. One who undertakes to discuss pornography finds himself, willy-nilly, falling back upon some of his ultimate positions in matters aesthetic, social, psychological, ethical. If a reader agrees with these opinions, he is likely to view them as principles; if he disagrees, prejudices. Here are some of mine.

Before plunging ahead, I had better indicate two mutually antagonistic dispositions, one liberal, the other conservative, in my opinions on pornography. On the one hand, I favor the liberal view that the less power the state and the police have over us private citizens the better, that the less the state concerns itself with the individual's thoughts, entertainments, and sexual actions the better, and that we should do what we can to keep from drifting toward totalitarianism. In other words, let us have no censorship because it strengthens the state, which is already too strong. Also let us have none because most of the things that in fact get censored are less harmful than some of the things that do not—for example, large-circulation newspapers and magazines. Society is harmed far less by the free circulation of a book like *Fanny Hill* than it is by routine and accepted practices of the daily sensationalist press: let a man inherit ten million dollars, pour acid on his wife, or win a Nobel Prize, and reporter and photographer are made to intrude upon him and his family and then to exhibit to public view in as gross a manner as possible his follies, shames, or just plain private affairs. Such invasions of privacy are not only allowed, they are allowed for the purpose of letting the public enjoy these same invasions vicariously, all in the name of freedom of the press. I believe that this accepted practice has done more damage to society as a whole and to its citizens individually than massive doses of the most depraved pornography could ever do. So much for my liberal views.

On the other hand, I favor the conservative view that pornography exists among us and is a social evil, though a small one. That is, in a good society of any sort I can imagine—not some daydream utopia where man is impossibly restored to sexual innocence but a society populated with recognizable, imperfectible men—in a good society there would be active opposition to pornography, which is to say, considerable firmness in the drawing of lines beyond which actions, words, and images are regarded as indecent. Furthermore, the opinion that pornography should not be restrained I regard as being commonly a symptom of doctrinaire liberalism and occasionally an evidence of destructive nihilism.

A liberal suspicion of censorship and a conservative dislike of pornography are not very compatible. Some sort of compromise is necessary if they are to live together. Their marriage will never be without tensions, but maybe the quarrel between them can be patched up well enough for practical purposes.

Originally the word pornography meant a sort of low erotic art, the writing of and about whores with the intention of arousing a man's lust so that he would go to a whore, but some centuries ago, the word, like the practice itself, came to include considerably more than aesthetic pandering. It has come to overlap with obscenity, which originally meant nothing more than the filthy. Obscenity still means that primarily, but notions about what is filthy have changed. Defecating and urinating, instead of being just low and uninteresting, came to be viewed as filthy, obscene, taboo. Apparently, down in the underworld of taboo, things and functions easily become tinged with sexuality, especially functions as near the genitals as urinating and defecating. In any case, since in common practice no clear distinction is made between pornography and obscenity, I am offering, for the sake of convenience, a definition in which the single word pornography is stretched to include most of obscenity. The definition is mine, but not just mine; it also reflects the usages and attitudes of my society.

Pornography is the representation of directly or indirectly erotic acts with an intrusive vividness which offends decency without aesthetic justification.

Obviously this definition does not just describe but also judges; quite as obviously it contains terms that need pinning down—decency, for example. But pornography is not at all a matter for scientific treatment. Like various other areas of sexual behavior in which society takes an unsteady, wary interest—homosexuality, for example, or fornication or nudity—pornography is relative, an ambiguous matter of personal taste and the consensus of opinion. The grounds for this definition are psychological, aesthetic, and political.

THE CRITERION OF DISTANCE

Psychologically, pornography is not offensive because it excites sexual desire; desire as such is a fine thing, and there are happy times and places when desire should be excited and gratified freely and fully; moreover, even in inappropriate times and places there is plenty of free-floating desire abroad in the world; it doesn't take pornography to excite excesses of desire among young men and women. Nor is pornography offensive because, in its perverted and scatological versions, it excites disgust; in the proper context disgust serves the useful function of turning us from the harmful. Psychologically, the trouble with pornography is that, in our culture at least, it offends the sense of separateness, of individuality, of privacy; it intrudes upon the rights of others. We have a certain sense of specialness about those voluntary bodily functions each must perform for himself—bathing, eating, defecating, urinating, copulating, performing the sexual perversions from heavy petting to necrophilia. Take eating, for example. There are few strong taboos around the act of eating; yet most people feel uneasy about being the only one at table who is, or who is not, eating, and there is an absolute difference between eating a rare steak washed down by plenty of red wine and watching a close-up movie of someone doing so. One wishes to draw back when one is actually or imaginatively too close to the mouth of a man enjoying his dinner; in exactly the same way one wishes to remove oneself from the presence of a man and woman enjoying sexual intercourse. Not to withdraw is to peep, to pervert looking so that it becomes a sexual end in itself. As for a close-up of a private act which is also revolting, a man's vomiting, say, the avoidance-principle is the same as for a close-up of steak-eating, except that the additional unpleasantness makes one wish to keep an even greater distance.

Pornography also raises aesthetic questions, since it exists only in art—in painting, literature, sculpture, photography, theater—and my definition implies that it is offensive aesthetically. The central aesthetic issue is not whether certain subjects and words should be taboo but what distance should be maintained between spectator and subject. Because of our desire to withdraw from a man performing private acts and our doubly strong desire to withdraw from a man performing acts which are not only private but also disagreeable or perverted, we wish aesthetically to remain at a certain distance from such acts when they are represented in art. Nothing whatever in human experience should, as such, be excluded from consideration in a work of art: not Judas betraying Christ nor naked starved Jews crowded by Nazi soldiers into a gas chamber nor a child locked by his parents in a dark closet for months till he goes mad nor a man paying a whore to lash him with barbed wire for his sexual relief nor even husband and wife making love.

Nothing human is alien to art. The question is only, how close? But the criterion of distance is an extremely tricky one. Aesthetically, one good way to keep a spectator at a distance from the experience represented by an image is to make the image artificial, stylized, not like us. If it is sufficiently stylized, it may be vivid and detailed and still keep a proper distance from the viewer. One would normally feel uneasy at being with a lot of men, women, and children engaged in every imaginable form of pleasurable erotic activity. Yet the vivid throngs of erotic statues on certain Indian temples create in the viewer no uneasiness but are simply delightful to look at. The viewer is kept at a considerable remove by the impossible poses and expressions of the statues; he cannot identify with the persons performing the acts. For the statues do not represent lustful, passionate, guilty, self-conscious, confused people like you and me, but pure beings to whom all things are pure, paradisal folk who are expressing their joy in generation and the body by erotic acts: these are stylized artifices of blessedness. Another way of keeping the spectator at a proper distance from a private experience is to give very little of it—make the image small, sketch it in with few details. One does not want to be close to a man while he is defecating nor to have a close-up picture of him in that natural, innocent act—not at all because defecating is reprehensible, only because it is displeasing to intrude upon. One would much rather have a detailed picture of a thief stealing the last loaf of bread from a starving widow with three children than one of Albert Schweitzer at stool. However, Brueghel's painting "The Netherlandish Proverbs" represents two bare rear ends sticking out of a window, presumably of people defecating into the river below, and one quite enjoys the sight—because it is a small part of a large and pleasant picture of the world and because the two figures are tiny, sketched in, far away.

To be sure, a satiric work of art may purposely arouse disgust in its audience. Even the breast of a healthy woman is revolting when inspected too closely, as Swift knew when he had tiny Gulliver revolted by every blemish on the breast of the Brobdingnagian wet nurse suckling the baby. Our revulsion at the description of her breast sticking out a good six feet, with a nipple half the size of a man's head, is necessary to Swift's satiric purposes, and it is kept within bounds by his reminding us that if proportions had been normal—if Gulliver and she had been about the same size—both he and we would have been pleased by the sight of her breast. When the artist's purpose goes to the limit of satire and he intends, as Swift does in the fourth book of *Gulliver's Trav-*

els, to disgust us with man as such, then he will force us right into the unpleasantly private, as Swift gets us to contemplate the Yahoos copulating promiscuously and lovelessly, besmeared with their own excrement. The aesthetic danger of such powerful evocations of disgust is that the audience may and often does turn not only against the object of the artist's hatred but also against the artist and work of art for having aroused such unpleasant emotions. Swift, just because he succeeds so powerfully, is often reviled for his misanthropy in the voyage to the Houyhnhnms; the fourth book of *Gulliver's Travels* is even called a product and proof of madness—which is convenient and safe, for of course the fantasies of a madman may be pathetic and scary but they don't apply to us, *we* are sane.

THE EROTIC USED—AND MISUSED

There is a special problem raised by realism, because it aims to present people as they actually are. How can a realistic artist be true to his subject if he is forbidden direct access to an area of human behavior which is of considerable importance? The aesthetic problem is for the realistic artist to represent these actions in such a way as to lead to understanding of the characters without arousing disgust against them or a prurient interest in their activities. When he can accomplish this very difficult feat, then he is justified in including in a realistic work of art representations that would otherwise be pornographic. Here are two instances of intimate erotic acts realistically represented, one of a kiss which is pornographic, the other of a copulation which is aesthetically justified and hence is not pornographic.

In the movie *Baby Doll,* made by Elia Kazan, a healthy young man and woman who desire one another embrace. By this point in the movie the spectator is convinced that their lust is powerful but banal, and a brief and somewhat distant shot of their embracing would adequately suggest to him how intensely they wanted to consummate their desire. Instead, he is subject to a prolonged series of images, especially auditory images, the effect of which is to arouse his own lust and/or disgust, to no aesthetic end. The kiss becomes so severed from characters and plot that the spectator does not care how the couple are related, but cares only that they are given over to desire, and he is encouraged by the very depersonalization of that desire to give himself over to a lust of his own. He may be excited to want some sort of sexual activity with the next available person, but, more probably, observing and sharing in that movie embrace becomes a kind of substitute sexual activity on the part of the spectator. For, just because the scene in *Baby Doll* arouses its spectator vicariously and in a theater, the chief appetite it whets is not for casual fornication but for more voyeurism—which is good at least for the movie business. Even if *Baby Doll* were a good work of art, as it surely is not, this episode in itself would remain aesthetically unjustified and therefore pornographic, and would merit censoring.

The other example of an intimately presented erotic act is from the novel *Pretty Leslie* by R. V. Cassill. The reader is given an emotionally intense account of a young man and woman copulating in an abnormal way; the man hurts the woman, and the reader understands how he does it and why she lets him do it. This would seem to be essentially pornographic, yet it is not. The art of this novel redeems its ugliness. The reader is not encouraged to use this episode as an incitement to casual fornication or voyeurism. Instead, what is aroused in him is a profound understanding of the characters themselves, of a kind he could have got in no other way. To understand what these people were like, how they were connected, and why they did what they did to each other, the reader must be close to them as they make love, and because he knows this is necessary for his understanding, he will not use either the episode or the whole novel for pornographic ends, unless he himself is already perverted. In *Baby Doll* a natural private act, by being brought close for no legitimate reason, excites an uneasy desire whose satisfaction can only be indiscriminate or perverse. In *Pretty Leslie* the account of an unnatural private act is not so close as to create disgust but is close enough to lead toward moral understanding and aesthetic satisfaction: there is no other possible way for the novelist to accomplish this legitimate end, and the emphasis he gives the episode is in proportion to its contribution to the whole novel.

The aesthetic problem has been stated succinctly by Jean Genet. As a professed immoralist and enemy of society, he has no compunction about using pornography and in fact he once made a pornographic movie. But as a writer, he has this to say about his art (in an interview in *Playboy* magazine for April 1954): "I now think that if my books arouse readers sexually, they're badly written, because the poetic emotion should be so strong that no reader is moved sexually. In so far as my books are pornographic, I don't reject them. I simply say that I lacked grace."

Nothing said thus far would justify legal suppression, official censorship. The effect of pornography in a work of art is aesthetically bad, but it is no business of the state to suppress bad art. The effect of pornography on an individual psyche is that of an assault, ranging in severity from the equivalent of a mere pinch to that of an open cut; but in the normal course of things one can avoid such assaults without much trouble, and besides the wounds they make are seldom very severe one by one, though they may be cumulatively. To be sure, there are people who want and need pornography just as there are those who want and need heroin, but such a secret indulgence is not in itself socially dangerous. Here again, the state has no business intruding: a man's soul is his own to pollute if he wishes, and it is not for the state to say, "Be thou clean, be thou healthy, close the bathroom door behind you." It is only when pornography becomes public that, like dope, it takes on a sufficiently political cast for censorship even to be considered. It is unlike dope in that it sometimes acquires political overtones by being used ideologically, when put in the service of nihilism.

But in one important respect it is like dope: it usually becomes public by being offered for sale, especially to the young.

SELL IT UNDER THE COUNTER

The classic example of pornography is a filthy picture: it is ugly; it is sold and displayed surreptitiously; it allows the viewer to intrude vicariously upon the privacy of others; it shows two or more men and women posing for money in front of a camera, in attitudes which sexual desire alone would lead them to assume in private if at all. An adult looking at such a picture is roused to an excitement which may lead either to revulsion or to satisfaction, but whatever his reaction, he should be left alone to decide for himself whether he wants to repeat the experience. The state has no legitimate political concern with his private vices. But the effect on young people of such a picture, and especially of a steady diet of such pictures, is another matter. A common argument against allowing young people to have unrestricted access to pornography runs somewhat as follows.

About sex the young are curious and uncertain and have very powerful feelings. A filthy picture associates sexual acts with ugly, vicarious, and surreptitious pleasure, and helps to cut sex off from love and free joy. At the most, one experience of pornography may have a salutary effect on the curious, uncertain mind of an adolescent. To be shown what has been forbidden might provide him a considerable relief, and if he has feared that he is warped because of his fantasies, he can see how really warped are those who act on such fantasies. Moreover, by his own experience he can learn why pornography is forbidden: experience of it is at once fascinating, displeasing, and an end in itself, that is to say, perverse. However, too many experiences with pornography may encourage the young to turn their fantasies into actions ("in dreams begin responsibilities") or to substitute fantasies for actions, and so may confirm them in bad habits.

Whatever the validity of this argument, it or something like it is the rationale by which our society justifies its strong taboo against exposing children to pornography. For my own part, I would accept the argument as mostly valid. The state has no business legislating virtue; indeed, one of the symptoms of totalitarianism is the persistent attempt of the state not just to punish its citizens for wrongdoing, but to change their nature, to make them what its rulers conceive to be good. But patently the state has the obligation to protect the young against the public acts of the vicious.

This means that, in the matter of the sale and display of pornography, the state, the apparatus of the law, should have two effective policies. It should strictly forbid making pornography accessible to the young: "No One Under 18 Admitted." But as for pornography for adults, the law should rest content with a decent hypocrisy: "Keep it out of the marketplace, sell it under the counter, and the law won't bother you."

An assumption underlying such policies is that a certain amount of official hypocrisy is one of the operative principles of a good society. It is hard to imagine a civilized society which would not disapprove of adultery, for the maintenance of the family as an institution is one of the prime concerns of society, and adultery threatens the family. Yet, on the other hand, imagine living in a country in which the laws against adultery were strictly enforced—the informing, spying, breaking in upon, denouncing, the regiment of self-righteous teetotalers. What is obviously needed here is what we have: unenforced laws. Only an all-or-none zealot fails to distinguish between the deplorable hypocrisy of a man deceiving his neighbors for his own gain and the salutary hypocrisy of a government recognizing the limits beyond which it should not encroach upon its individual citizens. Another assumption underlying these recommendations is that the censorship of simple pornography for adults will never be very effective. There is a steady demand for it, and it is not important enough to prosecute at much expense. The main function of laws against adult pornography is to express disapproval of it.

Clearly the logic of this argument leads to prohibiting certain books and works of art that are now legally available in some parts of the country. For example, in some localities the courts have refused to prohibit the sale of *Fanny Hill*. This refusal seems to me quite irresponsible on any grounds other than a general refusal to censor pornography, for by any meaningful definition *Fanny Hill* is pornographic. Such story as there is in the novel exists for no other purpose than to provide occasions for detailed accounts of sexual encounters, and these accounts are the only passages in the book with power to stir the reader's emotions. The characters are very simple types without intrinsic interest, and Fanny herself is little more than a man's fantasy of female complaisance and sexual competence. The one literary quality which has made the book celebrated is a certain elegance of style; compared to most simple pornography it reads like a masterpiece, but to anyone familiar with eighteenth-century English prose it reads like several other third-rate novels. Surely the world is not in such need of third-rate eighteenth-century English fictional prose as to allow this consideration alone to justify the public sale of a work of sheer pornography. What else would justify its sale is hard to imagine. To deny that the book is pornographic or to say that its literary value redeems its pornography, is to blur distinctions, and for an august court of law to do so is for the state to abrogate one of its functions. An essential and conservative function of the state is to say, "Thou shalt not," to formulate society's taboos. Unless I am seriously mistaken, in this instance the court, speaking for the state, has refused to draw a clear line which corresponds to society's actual customs. In our culture the place for nudists is in a nudist colony, not on the city streets, and the way to sell books like *Fanny Hill* is under the counter, not over it. In the name of enlightenment and sexual permissiveness, the state is violating an actual taboo, and the reaction to many such violations may very well be a resurgence of that savage fanaticism which burns books and closes theaters.

WHAT TO CENSOR, AND WHY

I am going to defer a consideration of the nihilistic use of pornography, which would logically come next, and instead look at certain borderline questions of enforcing censorship. The censoring of unquestionable pornography is of little interest; it pretty directly reflects what decent society considers indecent at a given time; it is custom in action. But the censorship of borderline pornography demands discrimination and philosophy, without which censorship can degenerate into puritanical repressiveness of the kind there has been quite enough of during the past two or three centuries.

Thus far, my argument on what to censor and why has led to a legal position which is at least within hailing distance of common practice in the United States now. To purveyors of raw pornography our practice says in effect: bother your neighbors, especially children, and you will be punished; leave others untroubled by your vice and you will be viewed with disapproval by the law but left alone. This attitude is fine till one gets down to cases, but once it is a matter of wording and enforcing a law, the question must be answered: how is one to distinguish between pornographic and decent art? Still, such lines must be drawn if there are to be laws at all, and they must, in the nature of things, be arbitrary. As I see it, a more manageable form of the question is this: who should do the censoring? Whatever the answer to this question may be, whatever the best method of censoring, one thing is clear—our present method is unsatisfactory.

As things stand, an object is banned as pornographic on the judgment of some official in customs or the postal service or else by some police officer prodded by a local zealot. In most cases this judgment presents little difficulty: even civil-liberty extremists who are opposed to all censorship on principle blanch when they are confronted with genuine hard-core pornography, the unarguably warped stuff, the bulk of the trade. But sometimes there is the question of assessing the value of a work of art, and for this task the bureaucrats and policemen who are presently empowered to decide are unqualified.

Should *Fanny Hill* be offered to the public freely? When society has said *no* for generations and when judges and literary critics cannot agree on the question, it is wrong to allow a police sergeant to decide the matter. If a duly constituted public authority says, *"Fanny Hill* shall not be sold in this state,"* then the policeman's duty is clear: arrest the man who displays it for sale. But to leave to bureaucrats and policemen the task of making all the delicate discriminations necessary in deciding whether the novel should be censored in the first place is genuinely irresponsible of society at large and of legislators in particular. To be sure, cases are brought to court. But the laws offer such vague guidance that far too much depends on the quirks of the judge or jury at hand. *No censorship might be preferable to what we have now.*

In fact, a strong case can be made for removing all censorship of pornography. Here are six arguments for abolishing censorship. The first three seem to me valid. (1) No law can be framed so as to provide a clear and sure guide to bureaucrat, policeman, judge, and jury. (2) It is very hard to demonstrate that pornography does in fact injure many people severely, even adolescents, for if the desire to break taboos is satisfied imaginatively, it is less likely to issue in antisocial acts. (3) The less power the state and the police have the better.

There are three further arguments against censorship which are commonly used but which I find less persuasive. (1) Decent citizens can by their very disapproval segregate pornography without assistance from the state. But, in an age as troubled as ours and with so much private indiscipline and theoretical permissiveness in sexual matters, there is little reason to suppose that the moral disapproval of decent citizens would actually stop the public distribution of pornography. (2) It is arguable that some people are rendered socially less dangerous by having their sexual tensions more or less satisfied by pornography, tensions which unrelieved might well lead to much more antisocial acts. True, but pornography, if it is to help those who need and use it, must be outside the law, clearly labeled *shameful;* if society has any respect for them, it will sternly assure them that what they are doing is nasty by passing a law against it, and then will pretty much leave them alone. (3) In the past, censorship has not succeeded in keeping books of literary value from being read but has only attached an unfortunate prurience to the reading of them. But the prurience attached to reading pornography derives less from breaking a law than from violating the taboo which caused the law to come into existence.

GOODMAN'S LOVELY DAYDREAMS

There is another argument, more important and erroneous than any of these six, which is commonly advanced in favor of abolishing censorship. It hinges on a mistaken liberal doctrine about the nature of sexual taboos. According to this doctrine, sexual taboos, like fashions in dress, are determined by local custom and have as little to do with morality as the kinds of clothes we wear. However—the argument goes—people frequently mistake these sexual taboos for ethical rules, and pass and enforce laws punishing those who violate the taboos. The result is a reduction of pleasure in sex and an increase of guilt, with an attendant host of psychological and social ills. The obvious solution is to abolish the taboos and so liberate the human spirit from its chief source of oppression and guilt. At the moment in America, this ultimately Rousseauistic doctrine finds extensive elaboration in the writings of Paul Goodman,* and is present to some degree in the writings of many other intellectuals.

It presents a considerable difficulty: by supposing that the

* See pp. 42–60.

potent and obscure emotions surrounding sexual matters de-
rive from unenlightened customs, it holds out the hope that
enlightened views can liberate us from those customs so that
sex in every form can become healthy and fun for all. This is
a cheery, optimistic view, not unlike the sweet hopefulness
of the oldfashioned anarchists who thought that all we have
to do, in order to attain happiness, is to get rid of governments so we may all express our essentially good nature unrestrained. Such ideas would show to advantage in a museum
of charming notions, along with phlogiston and the quarrel
about how many angels can dance on the head of a pin, but
turned loose in the world they sometimes cause a bit of trouble. Sexual anarchism, like political anarchism before it, is a
lovely daydream. But it has come to be a part of fundamental
liberalism, and so a part of the body of doctrines accepted by
more and more of the rulers of the nation. Conceivably the
First Amendment will be taken literally ("Congress shall
make no law . . . abridging the freedom of speech or of the
press") and many or all legal restraints against pornography
may in fact be removed. But I believe that so far from elim-
inating sexual taboos, such an official undermining of them
would only arouse the puritans to strengthen the bulwarks;
the taboos would be made more repressive than ever; and
many of the goods of liberalism would be wiped out along
with and partly because of this utopian folly. Decent people
had better learn how to censor moderately, or the licentiousness released by liberal zealots may arouse their brothers the
puritan zealots to censorship by fire.

A *civilized method of censoring is feasible.* One does not
have to imagine a utopian system of extirpating pornography through some sexual revolution—an Eden of erotic
innocence in which prohibitions will be unnecessary because
social relations will be as they should be. In our actual, historical United States, in which perversions and pornography
flourish, one can imagine a better method of restraining pornography, which is yet within the framework of our customs
and procedures. It would operate somewhat as follows.

All decisions about what is legally pornographic in any of

the arts are in the custody of boards of censors. A board is elected or appointed from each of three general categories of citizens: for example, a judge or lawyer of good repute; a professor of art, literature, or one of the humanities; and a social worker, psychologist, or clergyman. These are not exciting categories; but in them, if anywhere, are likely to be found citizens whose own opinions will reflect decent social opinion and who are also capable of making the various discriminations the task calls for. Obviously it is necessary to keep sexual anarchists off the board; just as a person is disqualified from serving as a juror in a murder case if he is against capital punishment, so one would be disqualified from serving on a board of censors if he were against censoring pornography.

A board of censors must never look to a set of rules of thumb for guidance—not, as now, to the quantity of an actress's body that must be covered. Is a burlesque dancer's breast indecent from the nipple down or is it only the nipple itself that offends? That way foolishness lies. Rather, the censors must look only to their own personal experience with a given work of art for only in such experience can art be judged. For this reason, the censors should be people for whom society's taboos are part of themselves, not something in a code external to them. No photograph, drawing, book, stage show, or moving picture is banned by the police except at the instruction of this board. Its decisions, like those of every quasi-official public agency, are subject to appeal to the courts, but the Supreme Court would do all it could to dodge such cases. *The banning is deliberately hypocritical: out of sight out of mind, so long as children are not molested.*

The aesthetic and moral principles guiding the board are roughly these: distance and effect. At the distance of a movie close-up, a kiss between husband and wife can be pornographic. If a child and adult are sitting side by side watching a stage performance of a witty Restoration comedy of adultery, they are at altogether different distances from the play, the adult closer than the child; but at a marionette performance of a fairy-tale melodrama they reverse distances, the child closer this time and the adult farther away. As for effect on the spectator, this consideration is only slightly less tricky than distance. The question to be asked is whether a story intrudes on the privacy of its characters in order to give the reader vicarious and perverse sexual excitement or in order to provide him with a sympathetic understanding which he could have got in no other way. These criteria of distance and effect—these rubber yardsticks—apply to the parts as well as to the whole, so that a novel or a movie of some aesthetic merit may be judged as censorable in part. In a movie the part is excisable with more or less aesthetic harm to the movie as a whole; with a book, if the board decides the gravity of the offense outweighs such literary excellence as the whole book may possess, the book is banned— not burned, just no longer offered for public sale.

The system is scarcely watertight; it presents plenty of opportunity for contradictions and revisions; it has tensions built into it. But it would not be likely to become troublesome politically; for, without strengthening the state, it provides a better way than the present one for our society to enforce certain inevitable taboos. Civilization behaves as though men were decent, in full knowledge that they are not.

A WEAPON OF NIHILISM

The last aspect of the subject I am going to deal with is the use of pornography as a weapon of nihilistic destruction, especially by two important writers currently using it in this manner, Genet and Henry Miller. Such a writer as William Burroughs is less important because more successful; that is to say, the very thoroughness of his solipsistic nihilism defeats his purpose, for finally his novels are not only repetitious and revolting but also pointless, so that their failure as art keeps them from being a threat to society.

In this general context, the term nihilism signifies a great deal more than it did originally. In Turgenev's *Fathers and Sons,* where the word was given political currency, nihilism was quite idealistic; it held that a given society (Russia, in that case) was so corrupt or wicked that it should be destroyed, but destroyed so that a better society could emerge from its ruins. Those nineteenth-century Russian nihilists were extreme revolutionists, and quite high-minded; they did not advocate murder but political assassination, not promiscuous lust but free love. Among us now, James Baldwin is rather like those oldfashioned nihilists; he preaches destruction in the name of love. To be sure, the images of sexual love Baldwin offers are at once vacuous and indecent, and the images of disgust and blame are strong. Still, compared to the thoroughgoing destructivists, he and his books are not so wild. They are tamable enough, at least, to become the fashion, for they are interpreted—against his intention, or at least against one of his intentions—as preaching little more than a local rebellion, the righting of the injustice which American Negroes have endured for so long. However, there is a nihilism which is not against this or that unjust society or social injustice but against society as such; its rage is not just political but metaphysical as well; and pornography is one of its weapons.

Genet sometimes strives to be this sort of nihilist. But in his best work, *The Balcony* especially, he is too good an artist to succeed as a total nihilist. *The Balcony* creates an imperfect but strong image of the corruptness of modern Western societies, a satiric exaggeration which the audience can recognize as the truth distorted mostly for dramatic effect. Genet the sexual pervert and social criminal sometimes wants to destroy society, though as a criminal of intelligence he knows that he needs the law his enemy; but as a dramatic artist he makes meaningful works which by their very structure oppose destruction. And the potential pornography of the works serves a dramatic end. Furthermore, he has made them to be presented in a theater, that most social of artistic forms. As a result, whatever Genet himself wants to say, a play such as *The Balcony* says to the audience, "Look how monstrously you have warped your society." So we look; and it is true, we have warped it monstrously. But this is moral art, this is not the assault of sheer nihilism. To see a performance of *The Balcony* drives one to serious contemplation of the nature of society and law. What this contemplation leads me to is the conclusion that we must improve our society and firm up our laws, for the alternatives that now appear to be open to us in the way of other social arrangements are not worth the agony and risk of attempting a revolution. The play docs not arouse a nihilistic zeal to destroy society, any more than it arouses sexual desire.

THE CASE OF HENRY MILLER

Of nihilistic fiction, Henry Miller's *Tropic of Cancer* is currently the most widely read and the best spoken of. Miller is not only a fairly good writer, but the personality he projects in his book is attractive. When he stands stripped of his civilization—stripped down to his language, that is—the savage that is left is not exactly noble but he is at least honest about himself, self-indulgent, energetic, beauty-loving, and interested in the world, not a cold-hearted, torturing pervert. The one overwhelming moral virtue Miller embodies in his book is self-honesty: if you're going to be a whore, he says, be a whore all the way. This honesty is doubtless what most attracted Orwell in Miller's writing, though Orwell was a most fastidious man otherwise. Miller's prose is usually vigorous and sometimes splendid, and he is the best writer of "the character" since Sir Thomas Overbury.

Should *Tropic of Cancer* be censored or not? According to the standards for censorship advanced earlier in my argument it should not be censored for its pornography: as a work of art, it has considerable merit, and it could not achieve its ends without the use of intrinsically pornographic episodes and images. But the conflict of interests in judging this book is acute, for the purpose of Miller's novel is not just aesthetic, it is nihilistic as well. The literary value of the book is enough to redeem its pornography but not enough to make one ignore its destructive intention. *Tropic of Cancer* has no structure and is very verbose; it is, like Miller's other books, an anatomy and a segment of his imaginary autobiography, a string of images and actions. But it does have an unmistakable message: society is intrinsically vile, let us return to the natural man. In effect, this return to nature means as little work as possible and lots of loveless sex. Miller has often been mispraised, for example by Karl Shapiro, for a supposedly pagan rejoicing in sex. Miller himself is honest about his intention. Again and again he represents the sexual antics of his characters as evidence of desperation, lurking behind which is the total despair of meaninglessness. He is what he says he is: an enemy not just of the badness of our society, not just of our specific society, but of society as such. To do what he can to get his readers also to become enemies of society, he assaults with persuasive force taboos, especially sexual taboos, which are intrinsic to social order.

Yet a whole new set of justifications is needed if *Tropic of Cancer* is to be banned, justifications having to do with pornography as a destructive social act. As an act against society, to write, publish, and distribute a book like *Tropic of Cancer* is more serious than to write, publish, and distribute a pamphlet which intellectually advocates the forcible overthrow of the government, but less serious than to take arms against the government—about on a par with inciting to rebellion, an act which a secure, free government will watch carefully and disapprove of strongly, but not forbid and punish. In other words, the only plausible argument for suppressing *Tropic of Cancer* would be that its publication is a dangerous political act and not that the book is pornographic, even though its pornography is the main instrument of the book's nihilistic force.

If you want to destroy society—not just write about a character who wants to, but if you want to make your book an instrument for destroying, a weapon—then you need pornography. For since society, at least Western society, is founded on the family as an essential social unit, nihilists and totalitarians must always attack the family as their enemy; conversely, those who attack the family as an institution are enemies of our kind of society. The totalitarians would substitute the state for the family; the nihilists would dissolve both the state and the family in the name of unrestricted gratification of natural appetite. To effect this dissolution, nihilists assault taboos, both because taboos restrain appetite and because they are an integral part of civilized order, of society as such. And since of all taboos the sexual ones are much the most important, pornography becomes for the nihilists (as it does not for the totalitarians, who need taboos) important as an instrument of dissolution; obviously a nihilistic representation of people violating taboos will be effective only if the representation itself also violates taboos. The reverse does not hold: pornography is not intrinsically nihilistic; conventional pornography recognizes and needs the rules it disobeys.

Because most pornography is not terribly harmful, and also because of the prevalence of liberal permissiveness in sexual matters, our society is falling down on one of its lesser jobs—the drawing of firm lines about what is decent. Furthermore, it has not sufficiently recognized that indecency can be and sometimes is put to politically dangerous uses. Society should oppose those who proclaim themselves its enemies and who subvert it by every means they know, not least of which is pornography. But violent repressiveness is not the best way for it to oppose them.

OUR LOST INNOCENCE

If one is for civilization, for being civilized, for even our warped but still possible society in preference to the anarchy that threatens from one side or the totalitarianism from the other, then one must be willing to take a middle way and to pay the price for responsibility. As things stand now, so liberal are we that a professor whose salary is paid by the state can speak out more easily in favor of *Tropic of Cancer* than against it, applauding not just its literary merits but also what he calls its celebration of sensuality and antisocial individualism. These are his honest opinions, and he, nor more than the book, should be censored for advancing them. But his colleagues should not allow themselves to be cowed by his scorn of what he calls their bourgeois respectability but should rise in opposition to those opinions. In Miller's own presentation, his sensuality would guard against despair but itself becomes a way to despair; his individualism is a frenzied endeavor to compose a self in the vacuum of alienation, an alienation which he childishly blames the absolute villain, society, for imposing on him, the absolute victim; he intends his book to be an instrument for persuading its readers to abandon society, abrogate responsibility to their fellow men, and revert to a parasitic life. He claims that this sensual life is more joyous and fulfilling than any other possible in civilization; but what he describes is not a sensuality which is indeed a fulfillment for adult persons, so much as a would-be consolation for those who aspire to the condition of babies as a remedy to their grown-up woe.

To be civilized, to accept authority, to rule with order, costs deep in the soul, and not least of what it costs is likely to be some of the sensuality of the irresponsible. (In this respect the politically repressed are irresponsible, being denied responsibility. This would help account for the apparently greater sensuality among American Negroes than among American whites, for as a group Negroes have only recently been allowed to assume much social responsibility.) But we Americans, black and white, must be civilized now whether we want to be or not. Perhaps before civilization savages were noble, but, if there is anything we have learned in this vile century, it is that those who regress from civilization become ignoble beyond all toleration. They may aspire to an innocent savagery, but what they achieve is brutality.

At the end of *Tropic of Cancer,* Henry Miller says: "Human beings make a strange flora and fauna. From a distance they appear negligible; close up they are apt to appear ugly and malicious." What Miller says is right enough, but he leaves out what matters most. There is a middle distance from which to look at a man, the flexible distance of decency and art, of civilized society, which defines both a man looking and a man looked at; and from this distance human beings can look pretty good, important, even beautiful sometimes, worthy of respect.

George Steiner

Night Words: High Pornography and Human Privacy

IS THERE ANY SCIENCE-FICTION PORNOGRAPHY? I MEAN SOME-
thing *new,* an invention by the human imagination of new
sexual experience? Science fiction alters at will the coordi-
nates of space and time; it can set effect before cause; it

[Controversy over this article continued for many months, and is continuing
still. My knowledge of and interest in pornography are, I would suppose, no
greater than the middle-class average. What I was trying to get into focus is
the notion of the "stripping naked" of language, of the removal from private, intensely privileged or adventurous use, of the erotic vocabulary. It
does seem to me that we have scarcely begun to understand the impoverish-
ment of our imaginings, the erosion into generalized banality of our resources of individual erotic representation and expression. This erosion is

works within a logic of total potentiality—"all that can be imagined can happen." But has it added a single item to the repertoire of the erotic? I understand that in a forthcoming novel the terrestial hero and explorer indulges in mutual masturbation with a bizarre, interplanetary creature. But there is no real novelty in that. Presumably one can use anything from seaweed to accordions, from meteorites to lunar pumice. A galactic monster would make no essential difference to the act. It would not extend in any real sense the range of our sexual being.

The point is crucial. Despite all the lyric or obsessed cant about the boundless varieties and dynamics of sex, the actual sum of possible gestures, consummations, and imaginings is drastically limited. There are probably more foods, more undiscovered eventualities of gastronomic enjoyment or revulsion than there have been sexual inventions since the Empress Theodora resolved "to satisfy all amorous orifices of the human body to the full and at the same time." There just aren't that many orifices. The mechanics of orgasm imply fairly rapid exhaustion and frequent intermission. The nervous system is so organized that responses to simultaneous stimuli at different points of the body tend to yield a single, somewhat blurred sensation. The notion (fundamental to Sade and much pornographic art) that one can double one's ecstasy by engaging in *coitus* while being at the same time deftly sodomized is sheer nonsense. In short: given the physiological and nervous complexion of the human body, the number of ways in which orgasm can be achieved or arrested, the total modes of intercourse, are fundamentally

very directly a part of the general reduction of privacy and individual style in a mass-consumer civilization. Where everything can be said with a shout, less and less can be said in a low voice. I was also trying to raise the question of what relation there *may* be between the dehumanization of the individual in pornography and the making naked and anonymous of the individual in the totalitarian state (the concentration camp being the logical epitome of that state). Both pornography and totalitarianism seem to me to set up power relations which must necessarily violate privacy.

Though the discussion which followed on publication has been heated, neither of these two issues has, I feel, been fully understood or engaged.]

finite. The mathematics of sex stop somewhere in the region of *soixante-neuf;* there are no transcendental series.

This is the logic behind the *120 Days.* With the pedantic frenzy of a man trying to carry *pi* to its final decimal, Sade labored to imagine and present the sum total of erotic combinations and variants. He pictured a small group of human bodies and tried to narrate every mode of sexual pleasure and pain to which they could be subject. The variables are surprisingly few. Once all possible positions of the body have been tried—the law of gravity does interfere—once the maximum number of erogenous zones of the maximum number of participants have been brought into contact, abrasive, frictional, or intrusive, there is not much left to do or imagine. One can whip or be whipped; one can eat excrement or quaff urine; mouth and private part can meet in this or that commerce. After which there is the gray of morning and the sour knowledge that things have remained fairly generally the same since man first met goat and woman.

This is the obvious, necessary reason for the inescapable monotony of pornographic writing, for the fact well known to all haunters of Charing Cross Road or pre-Gaullist bookstalls that dirty books are maddeningly the same. The trappings change. Once it was the Victorian nanny in high-button shoes birching the master, or the vicar peering over the edge of the boys' lavatory. The Spanish Civil War brought a plethora of raped nuns, of buttocks on bayonets. At present, specialized dealers report a steady demand for "WS" (stories of wife-swapping, usually in a suburban or honeymoon-resort setting). But the fathomless tide of straight trash has never varied much. It operates within highly conventionalized formulas of low-grade sadism, excremental drollery, and banal fantasies of phallic prowess or feminine responsiveness. In its own way the stuff is as predictable as a Boy Scout manual.

Above the pulp line—but the exact boundaries are impossible to draw—lies the world of erotica, of sexual writing with literary pretensions or genuine claims. This world is much larger than is commonly realized. It goes back to

Egyptian literary papyri. At certain moments in Western society, the amount of "high pornography" being produced may have equaled, if not surpassed, ordinary *belles-lettres*. I suspect that this was the case in Roman Alexandria, in France during the *Régence,* perhaps in London around the 1890's. Much of this subterranean literature is bound to disappear. But anyone who has been allowed access to the Kinsey library in Bloomington, and has been lucky enough to have Mr. John Gagnon as his guide, is made aware of the profoundly revealing, striking fact that there is hardly a major writer of the nineteenth or twentieth century who has not, at some point in his career, be it in earnest or in the deeper earnest of jest, produced a pornographic work. Likewise there are remarkably few painters, from the eighteenth century to post-Impressionism, who have not produced at least one set of pornographic plates or sketches. (Would one of the definitions of abstract, nonobjective art be that it cannot be pornographic?)

Obviously a certain proportion of this vast body of writing has literary power and significance. Where a Diderot, a Crébillon *fils,* a Verlaine, a Swinburne, or an Apollinaire write erotica, the result will have some of the qualities which distinguish their more public works. Figures such as Beardsley and Pierre Louÿs are minor, but their lubricities have a period charm. Nevertheless, with very few exceptions, "high pornography" is not of pre-eminent literary importance. It is simply not true that the locked cabinets of great libraries or private collections contain masterpieces of poetry or fiction which hypocrisy and censorship banish from the light. (Certain eighteenth-century drawings and certain Japanese prints suggest that the case of graphic art may be different; here there seems to be work of the first quality which is not generally available.) What emerges when one reads some of the classics of erotica is the fact that they too are intensely conventionalized, that their repertoire of fantasy is limited, and that it merges, almost imperceptibly, into the dream-trash of straight, mass-produced pornography.

In other words: the line between, say, *Thérèse Philosophe* or *Lesbia Brandon* on the one hand, and *Sweet Lash* or *The Silken Thighs* on the other, is easily blurred. What distinguishes the "forbidden classic" from under-the-counter delights on Frith Street is, essentially, a matter of semantics, of the level of vocabulary and rhetorical device used to provoke erection. It is not fundamental. Take the masturbating housemaid in a very recent example of the Great American Novel, and the housemaid similarly engaged in *They Called Her Dolly* (n.d., price six shillings). From the point of view of erotic stimulus, the difference is one of language, or more exactly—as verbal precisions now appear in high literature as well—the difference is one of narrative sophistication. Neither piece of writing adds anything new to the potential of human emotion; both add to the waste.

Genuine additions are, in fact, very rare. The list of writers who have had the genius to enlarge our actual compass of sexual awareness, who have given the erotic play of the mind a novel focus, an area of recognition previously unknown or fallow, is very small. It would, I think, include Sappho, in whose verse the Western ear caught, perhaps for the first time, the shrill, nerve-rending note of sterile sexuality, of a libido necessarily, deliberately, in excess of any assuagement. Catullus seems to have added something, though it is at this historical distance nearly impossible to identify that which startled in his vision, which caused so real a shock of consciousness. The close, delicately plotted concordance between orgasm and death in Baroque and Metaphysical poetry and art clearly enriched our legacy of excitement, as had the earlier focus on virginity. The development in Dostoevsky, Proust, and Mann of the correlations between nervous infirmity, the psychopathology of the organism, and a special erotic vulnerability, is probably new. Sade and Sacher-Masoch codified, found a dramatic syntax for, areas of arousal previously diffuse or less explicitly realized. In *Lolita* there is a genuine enrichment of our common stock of temptations. It is as if Vladimir Nabokov had brought into our field of vision what lay at the far edge, in Balzac's *La Rabouil-*

leuse, for instance, or what had been kept carefully implausible through disproportion (*Alice in Wonderland*). But such annexations of insight are rare.

The plain truth is that in literary erotica as well as in the great mass of "dirty books" the same stimuli, the same contortions and fantasies, occur over and over with unutterable monotony. In most erotic writing, as in man's wet dreams, the imagination turns, time and time again, inside the bounded circle of what the body can experience. The actions of the mind when we masturbate are not a dance; they are a treadmill.

Mr. Maurice Girodias would riposte that this is not the issue, that the interminable succession of fornications, flagellations, onanisms, masochistic fantasies, and homosexual punch-ups which fill his *Olympia Reader* are inseparable from its literary excellence, from the artistic originality and integrity of the books he published at the Olympia Press in Paris. He would say that several of the books he championed, and from which he has now selected representative passages, stand in the vanguard of modern sensibility, that they are classics of post-war literature. If they are so largely concerned with sexual experience, the reason is that the modern writer has recognized in sexuality the last open frontier, the terrain on which his talent must, if it is to be pertinent and honest, engage the stress of our culture. The pages of the *Reader* are strewn with four-letter words, with detailed accounts of intimate and specialized sexual acts, precisely because the writer has had to complete the campaign of liberation initiated by Freud, because he has had to overcome the verbal taboos, the hypocrisies of imagination in which former generations labored when alluding to the most vital, complex part of man's being.

> *Writing dirty books was a necessary participation in the common fight against the Square World . . . an act of duty.*

Mr. Girodias has a case. His reminiscences and polemics make sour reading (he tends to whine); but his actual pub-

lishing record shows nerve and brilliance. The writings of
Henry Miller matter to the history of American prose and
self-definition. Samuel Beckett's *Watt* appeared with Olympia, as did writings of Jean Genet, though not the plays or
the best prose. *Fanny Hill* and, to a lesser degree, *Candy,* are
mock-epics of orgasm, books in which any sane man will take
delight. Lawrence Durrell's *Black Book* seems to me grossly
overrated, but it has its serious defenders. Girodias himself
would probably regard *Naked Lunch* as his crowning dis-
cernment. I don't see it. The book strikes me as a strident
bore, illiterate and self-satisfied right to its heart of pulp. Its
repute is important only for what it tells us of the currents
of homosexuality, camp, and modish brutality which domi-
nate present "sophisticated" literacy. Burroughs indicts his
readers, but not in the brave, prophetic sense argued by Girodias. Nevertheless, there can be no doubt of the genuine-
ness of Girodias' commitment or of the risks he took.

Moreover, two novels on his list *are* classics, books whose
genius he recognized and with which his own name will remain proudly linked: *Lolita* and *The Ginger Man.* It is a
piece of bleak irony—beautifully appropriate to the entire
"dirty book" industry—that a subsequent disagreement
with Nabokov now prevents Girodias from including anything of *Lolita* in his anthology. To all who first met Humbert Humbert in *The Traveller's Companion Series,* a green
cover and the Olympia Press's somewhat mannered typogra-
phy will remain a part of one of the high moments of contemporary literature. This alone should have spared Mr. Girodias the legal and financial harryings by which Gaullist
Victorianism hounded him out of business.

But the best of what Olympia published is now available
on every drugstore counter—this being the very mark of
Girodias' foresight. The *Olympia Reader* must be judged by
what it actually contains. And far too much of it is tawdry
stuff, "doing dirt on life," with only the faintest pretensions
to literary merit or adult intelligence.

It is almost impossible to get through the book at all. Pick it up at various points and the sense of *déjà-vu* is inescapable ("This is one stag-movie I've seen before"). Whether a naked woman gets tormented in Sade's dungeons (*Justine*), during Spartacus' revolt (Marcus Van Heller: *Roman Orgy*), in a kinky French château (*Story of O*), or in an Arab house (*Kama Houri* by one Ataullah Mordaan) makes damn little difference. Fellatio and buggery seem fairly repetitive joys whether enacted between Paris hooligans in Genet's *Thief's Journal*, between small-time hustlers and ex-prize fighters (*The Gaudy Image*), or between lordly youths by Edwardian gaslight in *Teleny*, a silly piece attributed to Oscar Wilde.

After fifty pages of "hardening nipples," "softly opening thighs," and "hot rivers" flowing in and out of the ecstatic anatomy, the spirit cries out, not in hypocritical outrage, not because I am a poor Square throttling my libido, but in pure, nauseous boredom. Even fornication can't be as dull, as hopelessly predictable, as all that.

Of course there are moments which excite. *Sin for Breakfast* ends on a subtle, comic note of lewdness. *The Woman Thing* uses all the four-letter words and anatomical exactitudes with real force; it exhibits a fine ear for the way in which sexual heat compresses and erodes our uses of language. Those, and I imagine it includes most men, who use the motif of female onanism in their own fantasy life will find a vivid patch. There may be other nuggets. But who can get through the thing? For my money, there is one sublime moment in the *Reader*. It comes in an extract (possibly spurious?) from Frank Harris' *Life and Loves*. Coiling and uncoiling in diverse postures with two naked Oriental nymphets and their British procuress, Harris is suddenly struck with the revelation that "there indeed is evidence to prove the weakness of so much of the thought of Karl Marx. It is only the bohemian who can be free, not the proletarian." The image of Frank Harris, all limbs and propensities ecstatically engaged, suddenly disproving *Das Kapital* is worth the price of admission.

But not really. For that price is much higher than Mr. Girodias, Miss Mary McCarthy, Mr. Wayland Young, and other advocates of total frankness seem to realize. It is a price which cuts deep not only into the true liberty of the writer, but into the diminishing reserves of feeling and imaginative response in our society.

The preface to the *Olympia Reader* ends in triumph:

> *Moral censorship was an inheritance from the past, deriving from centuries of domination by the Christian clergy. Now that it is practically over, we may expect literature to be transformed by the advent of freedom. Not freedom in its negative aspects, but as the means of exploring all the positive aspects of the human mind, which are all more or less related to, or generated by, sex.*

This last proposition is almost unbelievably silly. What needs a serious inquiry is the assertion about freedom, about a new and transforming liberation of literature through the abolition of verbal and imaginative taboos.

Since the *Lady Chatterley* case and the defeat of a number of attempts to suppress books by Henry Miller, the sluice gates stand open. Sade, the homosexual elaborations of Genet and Burroughs, *Candy, Sexus, L'Histoire d'O* are freely available. No censorship would choose to make itself ridiculous by challenging the sadistic eroticism, the minutiae of sodomy (smell and all) which grace Mailer's *American Dream*. This is an excellent thing. But let us be perfectly clear why. Censorship is stupid and repugnant for two empirical reasons: censors are men no better than ourselves, their judgments are no less fallible or open to dishonesty. Secondly, the thing won't work: those who really want to get hold of a book will do so somehow. This is an entirely different argument from saying that pornography doesn't in fact deprave the mind of the reader, or incite to wasteful or criminal gestures. *It may, or it may not.* We simply do not have enough evidence either way. The question is far more intricate than many of our literary champions of total freedom would allow. But to say that censorship won't work and should not be asked to is *not* to say that there has been a liberation of literature, that the writer is, in any genuine sense, freer.

On the contrary. The sensibility of the writer is free where it is most humane, where it seeks to apprehend and re-enact the marvelous variety, complication, and resilience of life by means of words as scrupulous, as personal, as brimful of the mystery of human communication, as the language can yield. The very opposite of freedom is cliché, and nothing is less free, more inert with convention and hollow brutality, than a row of four-letter words. Literature is a living dialogue between writer and reader only if the writer shows a twofold respect: for the imaginative maturity of his reader, and, in a very complex but central way, for the wholeness, for the independence and core of life, in the personages he creates.

Respect for the reader signifies that the poet or novelist invites the consciousness of the reader to collaborate with his own in the act of presentment. He does not tell all because his work is not a primer for children or the retarded. He does not exhaust the possible responses of his reader's own imaginings, but delights in the fact that we will fill in from our own lives, from resources of memory and desire proper to ourselves, the contours he has drawn. Tolstoy is infinitely freer, infinitely more exciting, than the new eroticists when he arrests his narrative at the door of the Karenins' bedroom, when he merely initiates, through the simile of a dying flame, of ash cooling in the grate, a perception of sexual defeat which each of us can re-live or detail for himself. George Eliot is free, and treats her readers as free, adult human beings, when she conveys, through inflection of style and mood, the truth about the Casaubon honeymoon in *Middlemarch,* when she makes us imagine for ourselves how Dorothea has been violated by some essential obtuseness. These are profoundly exciting scenes, these enrich and complicate our sexual awareness, far beyond the douche-bag idylls of the contemporary "free" novel. There is no real freedom whatever in the compulsive physiological exactitudes of present "high pornography," because there is no respect for the reader, whose imaginative means are set at nil.

And there is none for the sanctity of autonomous life in the characters of the novel, for that tenacious integrity of existence which makes a Stendhal, a Tolstoy, a Henry James tread warily around their own creations. The novels being produced under the new code of total statement shout at their personages: strip, fornicate, perform this or that act of sexual perversion. So did the S.S. guards at rows of living men and women. The total attitudes are not, I think, entirely distinct. There may be deeper affinities than we as yet understand between the "total freedom" of the uncensored erotic imagination and the total freedom of the sadist. That these two freedoms have emerged in close historical proximity may not be coincidence. Both are exercised at the expense of someone else's humanity, of someone else's most precious right—the right to a private life of feeling.

This is the most dangerous aspect of all. Future historians may come to characterize the present era in the West as one of a massive onslaught on human privacy, on the delicate processes by which we seek to become our own singular selves, to hear the echo of our specific being. This onslaught is being pressed by the very conditions of an urban mass-technocracy, by the necessary uniformities of our economic and political choices, by the new electronic media of communication and persuasion, by the ever-increasing exposure of our thoughts and actions to sociological, psychological, and material intrusions and controls. Increasingly, we come to know real privacy, real space in which to experiment with our sensibility, only in extreme guises: nervous breakdown, addiction, economic failure. Hence the appalling monotony and *publicity*—in the full sense of the word—of so many outwardly prosperous lives. Hence also the need for nervous stimuli of an unprecedented brutality and technical authority.

Sexual relations are, or should be, one of the citadels of

privacy, the night place where we must be allowed to gather the splintered, harried elements of our consciousness to some kind of inviolate order and repose. It is in sexual experience that a human being alone, and two human beings in that attempt at total communication which is also communion, can discover the unique bent of their identity. There we may find for ourselves, through imperfect striving and repeated failure, the words, the gestures, the mental images which set the blood to racing. In that dark and wonder ever renewed both the fumblings and the light must be our own.

The new pornographers subvert this last, vital privacy; they do our imagining for us. They take away the words that were of the night and shout them over the rooftops, making them hollow. The images of our love-making, the stammerings we resort to in intimacy, come prepackaged. From the rituals of adolescent petting to the recent university experiment in which faculty wives agreed to practise onanism in front of the researchers' cameras, sexual life, particularly in America, is passing more and more into the public domain. This is a profoundly ugly and demeaning thing whose effects on our identity and resources of feeling we understand as little as we do the impact on our nerves of the perpetual "sub-eroticism" and sexual suggestion of modern advertisement. Natural selection tells of limbs and functions which atrophy through lack of use; the power to feel, to experience and realize the precarious uniqueness of each other's being, can also wither in a society. And it is no mere accident (as Orwell knew) that the standardization of sexual life, either through controlled license or compelled puritanism, should accompany totalitarian politics.

Thus the present danger to the freedom of literature and to the inward freedom of our society is not censorship or verbal reticence. The danger lies in the facile contempt which the erotic novelist exhibits for his readers, for his personages, and for the language. Our dreams are marketed wholesale.

Because there were words it did not use, situations it did

not represent graphically, because it demanded from the reader not obeisance but live echo, much of Western poetry and fiction has been a school to the imagination, an exercise in making one's awareness more exact, more humane. My true quarrel with the *Olympia Reader* and the *genre* it embodies is not that so much of the stuff is boring and abjectly written. It is that these books leave a man less free, less himself, than they found him; that they leave language poorer, less endowed with a capacity for fresh discrimination and excitement. It is not a new freedom that they bring, but a new servitude. In the name of human privacy, enough!

Kenneth Tynan

Dirty Books Can Stay

IT'S ALWAYS PLEASANT TO SEE PRUDERY KNOCKED, AND WHEN-
ever I read articles by fellow-intellectuals in defense of pornography, I do my best to summon up a cheer. Lately, however, the heart has gone out of my hurrahs. The old adren-
alin glow has waned. And now that I've analyzed a number
of recent anti-censorship tracts, I think I know why. *The
writers are cheating.* A whiff of evasiveness, even of outright
hypocrisy, clings to their prose: too much is left unspoken,
or unadmitted. Their arguments, when you look at them
closely, shift on the quicksands of timidity. On the surface, a

fearless libertarian has come forth to do battle with the forces of reaction. But between the lines he is usually saying something like this:

(a) I hate censorship in all its forms, but that doesn't mean that I actually like pornography.

(b) In fact, I don't even approve of it, except when I can call it "erotic writing" and pass it off as literature.

(c) I wouldn't go into a witness box to defend it unless it had educational, artistic or psychiatric value to make it respectable.

(d) I read it only in the line of duty, and feel nothing but pity for those who read it for pleasure.

(e) Needless to say, I never masturbate.

Such—once you've stripped off the rhetoric—is the accepted liberal viewpoint; and safer than that you can hardly play. At best, it adds up to a vaguely progressive gesture that could never endanger the author's moral standing or give his wife a moment's worry. From first to last he remains socially stainless and—to me, anyway—utterly unreal. He is like a man who loathes whorehouses in practice but doesn't mind defending them in principle, provided that they are designed by Mies van der Rohe and staffed by social workers in Balenciaga dresses.

At this point I had better offer a definition. By pornography I mean writing that is exclusively intended to cause sexual pleasure. I am not talking about novelists like D. H. Lawrence or Henry Miller; sex is often their theme, but titillation is never their main objective, and if they happen to arouse us, we keep ourselves resolutely zipped, aware that what we are feeling is only an incidental part of a large literary design. (This, of course, can be fairly frustrating at times. In *Lady Chatterley's Lover,* for instance, Lawrence has a teasing habit of getting the reader tumescent and suddenly changing the subject from sex to the dreadful side effects of the Industrial Revolution). Nor am I concerned with the Anglo-Saxon exiles in Paris who used to concoct spare-time pornography under pseudonyms for the Olympia Press; straight smut wasn't their métier, and too often they strayed from the purpose at hand into irrelevant gags and other flights of asexual fancy. *Candy,* by Terry Southern and Mason Hoffenberg, is a brilliant example of pseudo-pornography, praised by the liberal critics precisely because it was too funny to be sexy. As the porter in *Macbeth* said of drink: "It provokes the desire, but it takes away the performance."

What we are discussing is something different— hard-core pornography, which is orgasmic in intent and untouched by the ulterior motives of traditional art. It has a simple and localized purpose: to induce an erection. And the more skillfully the better. Contrary to popular myth, it takes discipline and devotion to be a first-rate pornographer, and only the subtlest command of rhythm and repetition will produce ideal results. These usually take the form of solo masturbation—usually, but not invariably, since vocal excerpts from bawdy books can often by employed to vary or intensify the customary fun of sexual coupling. In any case, the aim of pornography is physical enjoyment. Yet the liberals, at heart, disdain it, and the public as a whole seems eager to burn it. I think it deserves a few words of exculpation and thanksgiving.

In 1962 John Osborne wrote a short and startling play called *Under Plain Cover.* It dealt with a happily married suburban couple named Jenny and Tim, whose private life is entirely given up to the acting out of sexual fantasies. Sometimes she dresses up as a nurse, and he plays the apprehensive patient; in another version of the game he is a strict master threatening to punish a slovenly housemaid. They are both obsessed by Victorian knickers (English for panties), of which they have a unique collection. After one fetishistic session, they meditate as follows:

> *Jenny: Do you think there are many people like us?*
> *Tim: No. Probably none at all, I expect.*
> *Jenny: Oh, there must be some.*
> *Tim: Well, yes, but probably not two together.*
> *Jenny: You mean just one on their own?*
> *Tim: Yes.*
> *Jenny: How awful. We are lucky.*

Pornography is expressly designed for those who are not, in Jenny's sense, "lucky." If your taste is for earrings or high heels or spanking or any of the other minority appetites, you may have trouble finding a like-minded bedfellow. You will be "one on their own," and that can create a strangulating sense of guilt. Pornography loosens the stranglehold and assuages the solitude; you know, at least, that you are not alone. Having bought a book that matches your fantasy, you emerge from the store with a spring-heeled stride and a surge of elation. I have felt that radiant contentment, and so have you—*hypocrite lecteur, mon semblable, mon frère.* If chance denies you the right partner, that book and others like it will be your lifelong companions. Just as old habits die hard, old hards die habits.

The erotic minority man is not alone in needing the aid and comfort of pornography. Worse by far is the plight of those who are villainously ugly and unable to pay for the services of call girls. (If they are rich, their problem is negligible; beauty, after all, is in the eye of the stockholder.) To be poor and physically unappetizing is to be sexually condemned to solitary confinement, from which pornography offers the illusion of release. And we mustn't overlook its more commonplace uses. For men on long journeys, geographically cut off from wives and mistresses, pornography can act as a portable memory, a welcome shortcut to remembered bliss, relieving tension without involving disloyalty. And for uncommitted bachelors, arriving alone and short of cash in foreign cities where they don't speak the language, hard core is practically indispensable.

It's difficult to be an enemy of pornography without also disapproving of masturbation. In order to condemn the cause, it is logically necessary to deplore the effect. A century ago, when it was generally believed that self-stropping led to loss of hair, blindness and mental paralysis, I could have understood this attitude. Nowadays, I find it as baffling and repugnant as when I first encountered it, at the age of fourteen. The debating society at my school was discussing the motion: "That the present generation has lost the ability to entertain itself." Rising to make my maiden speech, I said with shaky aplomb: "Mr. Chairman—as long as masturbation exists, no one can seriously maintain that we have lost the ability to entertain ourselves." The teacher in charge immediately closed the meeting. Today his successor would probably take a more tolerant view. But the old prohibitions still persist. In a recent letter to the London *Sunday Times,* a respected liberal clergyman wrote: "To be sexually hungry is the fate of thousands, both young and old. There is nothing evil in this hunger, but it is hard to bear. To have it stimulated when it cannot be honorably satisfied is to make control more difficult."

Here, in three short sentences, all the puritan assumptions are on parade—that sexual deprivation is the normal state of affairs, that it is morally desirable to grin and bear it, and that masturbation is a dishonorable alternative.

Because hard core performs an obvious physical function, literary critics have traditionally refused to consider it a form of art. By their standards, art is something that appeals to such intangibles as the soul and the imagination; anything that appeals to the genitals belongs in the category of massage. What they forget is that language can be used in many delicate and complex ways to enliven the penis. It isn't just a matter of bombarding the reader with four-letter words. As Lionel Trilling said in a memorably sane essay on the subject:

> *I see no reason in morality (or in aesthetic theory) why literature should not have as one of its intentions the arousing of thoughts of lust. It is one of the effects, perhaps one of the functions, of literature to arouse desire, and I can discover no ground for saying that sexual pleasure should not be among the objects of desire which literature presents to us, along with heroism, virtue, peace, death, food, wisdom, God, etc.*

That is the nutshell case for pornography as art. It could hardly be stated more concisely, and I have yet to hear it

convincingly refuted. If a writer uses literary craft to provoke sexual delight, he is doing an artist's job. It is for him
to decide whether four-letter words will help or hinder his
design. C. S. Lewis, a great literary critic and Christian apologist, once jolted me by saying that he objected to venereal
monosyllables mainly because they were antiaphrodisiac;
from antiquity onward, the best writers had found that the
oblique approach to sex paid higher erotic dividends. ("The
direct approach," he told me, "means that you have to resort
to the language of the nursery, the gutter or the medical
textbook. And these may not be the associations you wish to
evoke.") But that is a question of taste. Whatever technique
the writer employs, we are entitled to judge the end product as a work of art. And the basic criterion, in the case of
pornography, is whether or not it succeeds in exciting us. If
it doesn't, we can write it off as an artistic failure.

Lawyers, as I discovered a couple of years ago, are not impressed by the Trilling doctrine. The English distributors of
Fanny Hill were being prosecuted for obscenity, and the
publisher's legal advisers asked me whether I would appear
as a witness for the defense. I said I'd be delighted. And
what form (they enquired) would my evidence take? I re-
plied by pointing out that under English law obscenity is
permissible as long as it has redeeming artistic merits; I considered erotic titilation a legitimate function of art, and
therefore proposed to defend *Fanny Hill* on the ground that
it was expertly titillating. The lawyers' professional smiles
froze on their faces. They didn't exactly throw me out, but
they made it arctically clear that I would not be called on to
testify. In terms of courtroom tactics, they may have been
right; it's just conceivable, however, that they missed a
chance of establishing (or at least of testing) a new legal precedent. In any event, they lost the case.

But I mustn't lurch into the trap of suggesting that pornography is defensible only when it qualifies as art. It is defensible in its own right and for its own sake, no matter
whether it is art or not, and whether it is well or badly writ-

ten. Freedom to write about sex must include the freedom to write about it badly. Some of the younger critics—guerrillas at the gates of the literary Establishment—would go further and argue that pornography is not only different from art but in some respects more important. A reviewer in *The International Times,* London's underground newspaper, recently declared:

> *In the brave new world of sexuality, perhaps we can forget about art, and read Henry Miller as he was meant to be read: as the writer whose craft describes intercourse better than anybody else's. If we have learned nothing else from Genet, we can be sure of this: his result may have been art, but that's not as important as his intention, which was pornography.*

Very few critics, even today, can write about hard core without tremors of prejudice and preconception. You can sense them worrying all the time about what their readers will think of them; it mustn't be suspected that they enjoy it, because that would imply that they masturbate. So they get defensively jocose, or wearily condescending. They indulge in squirms of pity for those who actually go out and buy the stuff—the sort of pity that is twin brother of contempt. Of course, the hellfire preachers of popular reviewing don't bother with such petty qualms; for them, all pornography is subversive filth and ought to be destroyed unread. It's only in the work of intelligent critics that you hear the special tone of veiled liberal distaste, which is rather like that of a lecturer on toxicology who feels compelled to reassure us, every few seconds, that he has never actually poisoned anyone. This tone is audible even in *The Other Victorians* by Steven Marcus, a much-praised and often perceptive study of pornography in nineteenth-century England. The author is an Associate Professor of English at Columbia. Let me list some of the errors, ambiguities and critical confusions that I detect in his book:

(1) Overdependence on Freudian dogma. Professor Marcus prefaces his text with the famous quotation in which

Freud proclaims that "the grandest cultural achievements
. . . are brought to birth by every greater sublimation of the
components of the sexual instinct." In other words, the less
energy you invest in sex, the more likely you are to produce
a work of art. This is a hypothesis with no scientific basis of
any kind. It is rather like saying that if you hoard enough
milk, it may somehow turn into wine. The whole theory
reeks of hidden puritanism, not to say magic.

(2) Overaddiction to Freudian symbolism. Describing a
Victorian handbook on pornography, Professor Marcus
points out that its author often hangs a page of footnotes
onto a single line of text. He adds that "one is tempted" to
see in this "an unconscious iconography: beneath a very
small head there is attached a very large appendage." Resist
the temptation, Marcus: this is sub-Freudian tittering at its
coyest. Later on, the professor quotes from a pornographer
who casually, and to avoid repeating himself—uses the
word "evacuation" to mean ejaculation. "If one expands the
metaphor," Marcus comments with poleaxing pedantry,
"one begins to see that the penis then might be either a fecal
column or the lower end of the alimentary tract out of
which fecal matter is to be expelled, the woman's body, particularly her genitals, becomes a toilet, etc." Watch out for
expanding metaphors, Marcus, especially if they're anal.
Again, when a hard-core hero, busily undressing a girl, says
that he "unveiled beauties enough to bring the dead to life,"
the professor insists that the phrase is an unconscious reference to the author and his readers: *they* are the dead who
need to be brought to life. If clichés can legitimately yield
interpretations like that, we enter a minefield every time we
uncover our typewriters.

(3) Verbal snobbery—*i.e.,* the assumption that the sexual
act is inherently too ignoble to be described in noble words.
When a pornographer writes about "that inner sovereignty
or force, within my balls," Marcus gets witheringly scornful:
"An 'inner sovereignty' that is yet 'within my balls' is hope-
less and impossible. Sovereignty is toppled from its throne

by being so located—there is nothing majestic about such an urgency." This reminds me of a telling exchange at the Old Bailey in 1960, when *Lady Chatterley's Lover* was being tried for obscenity. Counsel for the prosecution, an Old Etonian and veteran of the Coldstream Guards, read a passage from the novel in tones of frigid derision and then asked Richard Hoggart, a young scholar giving evidence for the defense, whether he seriously contended that it was possible to feel "reverence for a man's balls." "Indeed, yes," said Hoggart, with quiet compassion for the fellow's obtuseness. He made it seem so obvious; and as he spoke you could feel the case swinging in Lawrence's favor.

(4) Facile generalization, based on sloppy research. This crops up in the brief, disdainful chapter that Marcus devotes to the vast Victorian literature of flagellation. In books of this genre, he says, "what goes on is always the same. A person is accused of some wrongdoing. This person is most often a boy. . . . The accuser is almost invariably some surrogate for his mother. . . . An adult male figure, father or schoolmaster, occurs very infrequently." In fact, the victim is usually a girl, and male accusers are just as common as female. The professor's reading list must have been curiously selective.

(5) Moral censure masquerading as stylistic disapproval. Marcus has a habit of attacking pornography in particular on grounds that apply to literature in general. At one point, for instance, he quotes a sentence that makes cloudy use of epithets such as "voluptuous," "amorous" and "tumultuous." He goes on to say that, because they are vague and unspecific, "they express an important tendency in pornography." Nothing of the sort: what they express is a tendency that exists in bad writing of any kind. Foggy prose is no more abhorrent in pornography than in Norman Vincent Peale.

But for all his lapses, Marcus is at least trying to be an objective witness, and often he succeeds. The roughest frontal assault on hard core in recent years has come from George Steiner, a sprightly American don who teaches at Churchill College, Cambridge. It was launched in an essay called "Night Words," * which Steiner contributed to the English magazine *Encounter*. He begins by contending that, since the number of sexual positions and combinations is limited, pornography is doomed to ultimate monotony. To which one replies that dawn and sunset are likewise limited, but that only a limited man would find them monotonous.

Already, quite early in the piece, there are signs that Steiner is easily bored. With a stoic yawn, he says that after any kind of sexual fulfillment "there is the grey of morning and the sour knowledge that things have remained fairly generally the same since man first met goat and woman." (Why grey instead of flesh-pink? Why sour rather than sweet? Why goats anyway?) Hereabouts he takes a sudden swerve that brings him into head-on collision with Professor Marcus, who is approaching from the opposite direction. According to Steiner, one of the definitions of abstract art is "that it cannot be pornographic." According to Marcus, pornography is "in reality very abstract."

Steiner now zeros in on his target. Reasonably enough, he maintains that there is no essential difference between "erotic writing" and hard core except in the matter of verbal sophistication. But from this he argues that neither category "adds anything new to the potential of human emotion; both add to the waste." An assumption is buried here, and I trust you dig it: what Steiner means by waste is masturbation. A long passage follows in which he easily demolishes the pretensions of Maurice Girodias, founder of the Olympia Press, who is forever protesting that what he published was not pornography but art. (My own complaint would be that although it was sometimes good art, it was always lousy pornography.) This section is dotted with words like "bore," "boredom," "repetitive" and "dull," just in case you are in any doubt about Steiner's attitude toward the desirability of writing about physical love-making. For what he is leading up to is nothing less than blanket condemnation of all at-

* See pp. 96–108.

tempts to put the sexual act into words. He asserts that the best novelists leave sex in the wings; they stop at the bedroom door. To support his case he cites Tolstoy and George Eliot, both of whom lived at a time when it was forbidden to go further. As for modern outspokenness: "There is no real freedom whatever in the compulsive physiological exactitudes of present 'high pornography,' because there is no respect for the reader whose imaginative means are set at nil." Sex is a private citadel to be jealously guarded, an experience in which two human beings must find for themselves the mental images that will set their blood to racing in dark and wonder ever renewed. (I am compressing, but not all that much.) "The new pornographers," Steiner warns us dourly, "subvert this last, vital privacy; they do our imagining for us."

They do our imagining for us. It sounds like a fearful affront, a chilling premonition of 1984; but in fact it is exactly what all good writers have done since the birth of literature. The measure of their talent has immemorially been their ability to make us see the world through their eyes. If they can heighten our perceptions, we should thank them, not resent them. And on the matter of privacy: I don't think Steiner is seriously suggesting that commando groups of scribbling *voyeurs* are going to burst into our bedrooms and take notes. We can always keep our sex lives to ourselves if we wish. But that doesn't mean (why should it?) that we must shrink from reading about other people's.

Steiner's climactic point is that hard core has no respect for "the sanctity of autonomous life" as far as its characters are concerned. They don't exist in their own right, independent and self-sustaining, like people in Stendhal and Henry James. Pornographers, he says, "shout at their personages: strip, fornicate, perform this or that act of sexual perversion." The error here is one we have already noted in Marcus: Steiner is damning bad pornography for a crime that it shares with all bad fiction. Incompetent writers *always* shout at their characters: drink, take dope, perform this or that act of psychological perversion. In good pornography, as in good writing of any kind, the characters need no such external prompting. But Steiner goes on to compare pornographers with S.S. guards, who barked their orders at living men and women: "The total attitudes are not, I think, entirely distinct. There may be deeper affinities than we as yet understand between the 'total freedom' of the uncensored erotic imagination and the total freedom of the sadist. That these two freedoms have emerged in close historical proximity may not be coincidence."

But have they? History refutes the argument. Sadists were indulging their grisly whims centuries before the modern era of sadistic pornography. Slaughter for fun is not a recent invention. Gilles de Rais was exploiting it to the full long before the Marquis de Sade began his missionary activities; like all enthusiasts of his kind, in whatever period, Gilles needed sadistic books to inflame him about as much as a Madras curry needs a pepper mill.

The question of banning de Sade has been urgently debated in England ever since the Moors Murder trial in 1966, at which a neofascistic Scot named Ian Brady and his mistress, Myra Hindley, were sentenced to life imprisonment for a series of explicitly sadistic killings. Their victims were a seventeen-year-old youth and two children aged ten and twelve. Among the books found in Brady's lodgings was a study of the life and ideas of the Marquis de Sade. Did it supply him with fantasy scenarios which he later enacted in reality? Was this a case of life imitating art? Pamela Hansford Johnson, the novelist and wife of C. P. Snow, suspects that it might have been, and has poured her qualms into an agitated little book called *On Iniquity*. In it she comes out strongly against the free dissemination of pornography. "There is a tyranny of libertarianism as well as of restriction," she says, "and we can already hear its baying, and the rolling of its tumbrils." Miss Hansford Johnson is no professional bigot; she is a decent liberal in a state of sincere unease; but a cool survey of the facts suggests that her natural horror at the Brady-Hindley crimes has carried her to irrational extremes. Brady's record shows that he was cutting up live cats with a flick knife at the age of ten; and around the same time he tied up a school friend and tried to burn him to death. He was a practicing sadist before he ever heard of de Sade.

To my mind, the really evil books about physical cruelty are those which give it a moral justification. I am thinking, for example, of those Catholic tracts that appeared at the bloody high noon of the Inquisition, telling true believers that it was necessary to maim and incinerate unrepentant heretics for the good of their souls. I think, too, of military manuals on the use of bayonets and small arms, which teach you how to inflict the most refined and crippling pain for the greater good of your country. I despise such books and regret that there are people who like to read them. But I would not ban them.

One inalienable right binds all mankind together—the right of self-abuse. That—and not the abuse of others— is what distinguishes the true lover of pornography. We should encourage him to seek his literary pleasure as and where he finds it. To deny him that privilege is to invade the deepest privacy of all.

Ernest van den Haag

The Case for Pornography Is the Case for Censorship and Vice Versa

IMPULSIVELY, I AM AGAINST BOTH CENSORS AND PORNOGRA-phers—but even more against one without the other; if you are for either you should be for both. On reflection, I am: both are wanted and they call for each other, as toreros and bulls do, or hunters and game.

Pornography is sought eagerly at some times by many people and fervently at all times by some people. It is exciting and, perhaps, gratifying to those who seek it (to some of them nothing else is). I see no reason to grudge them their pleasures, squalid as they are. Nor am I upset by those who make their living supplying the materials, as long as they do so without soliciting obnoxiously. Censorship makes sure of that. And it also protects vulnerable people from injury or, at least, from distressing shocks to their sensibilities; perhaps, too, it provides self-righteous exaltation (or diversion) to the censors—which I do not begrudge either, however pretentious or grubby it be.

Pornography exhilarates and solaces some people, while censorship satisfies, relieves and shelters others. The world would be poorer without either. One may even argue, correctly I think, that, as it screens pornography from those who would be pained or offended by it, censorship also heightens the heady sensation of those who nevertheless get hold of what they crave—which, after all, is usually quite possible. Isn't the thrill, the excitement, the rapture of pornography associated with, if not altogether dependent on, its being forbidden? Wouldn't its piquancy be blunted were it officially tolerated or sanctioned? The shock value even of casual "dirty" words depends on their not becoming "clean" by approved or habitual public use.* It is the social taboo, legally endorsed, that gives pornography much of its defiant charm, and causes aficionados to be stirred—whether they root for the dark, ferocious bull or for the torero clad in his suit of light.

To be sure, neither side acknowledges its implicit need of the other; neither will give away the game since both enjoy it more by clinging to their conviction that it is not a game. Instead, each strains to make its motive unrecognizable by draping ornate and fusty pomposities over it: freedom and art on one side and, on the other, decency and the protection of women and children. Although occasionally pertinent, these travesties are nearly always pretense, and usually irrelevant. To me the pornography fanciers who oppose cen-

*The legal defense of risqué nightclub performers—that they do not go beyond "community standards"—is clearly absurd. People come to hear them go beyond. The only question is how far beyond they should be allowed to go, and, if we disregard the law as it now stands, whether, where, to what extent and how the law should enforce any limits.

sorship sound remarkably like masochists complaining about the pain on which their pleasure depends; and the censors seem to relish the proceedings no less.

One may compare censorship and pornography to fashion and nudity. As fashion does with a woman's actual body, so censorship covers some of the sexual components of her image. The prude feels protected from shock, the aesthete from ugliness, the anxious person from what he had to repress. But the defense is ambivalent. Quite as effectively as fashion, though less deliberately, censorship attracts attention and adds interest to what it conceals. An image may be censored because too prurient. But things also become prurient because censored. Fashion similarly covers an erotically significant portion of the body—or makes it erotically enticing by covering it.

Women certainly would be less alluring if they were always and fully bared to an indifferent eye. Selective covering makes prospects more enchanting: men want to see what women want to hide if only to make men want to see it—there can be no revelation if the truth is always naked, and no discovery. It is hardly sporting then to complain about the obstacles in a cross-country race, not very clever to announce that the goal could be reached faster by freeway: fashion or censorship provide a veil at once protective and alluring. Without them we might be shorn of longing.

There are broader reasons for censorship, too. Unless pornographers are restrained, the ethos of society may be eroded. However "pluralistic" or "individualistic" it preens itself on being, any society and all social bonds ultimately rest on a community of shared values. The values shared are different in each society. But unless it holds in common the values important to it, no culture can grow, no society persist. It happens that the values we share with respect to sex are important to us and set limits to the impulse to depict it, which we also share. The boundaries are watched over by censorship. They are changeable, of course, and have changed often. So has censorship.

But such changes are the products of changes in social values—not the producer. Nor are they generated by rational argument or by attempting to apply abstractly venerated general principles such as "freedom of expression." Indeed such general principles can be sustained only if they are not uniformly applied to all areas of human activity (they never were). Censorship thus will change, as does fashion. But both will remain as long as common values do, and remain capricious, for they are impelled by changing feelings rather than practical advantages which can be rationally calculated.

Further, if pornography were allowed to proliferate unchecked, it might influence both public and private attitudes and sensibilities, and, therefore, ultimately actions. For it is not true, Jimmy Walker notwithstanding, that "no girl has ever been ruined by a book." Whether a man tries to "ruin" a girl, and by what means he succeeds or fails, both his character and hers, and their ideas, ideals, and activities, are strongly influenced by the written word—even if neither actually reads. Jimmy Walker no doubt owed a great deal to the Bible—as it was interpreted to him—and Mme. Bovary or Mme. de Beauvoir a great deal to the books they read. There is reason to believe that the sadistic "moor murders" in England were rationalized and possibly inspired by the published fantasies of the Marquis de Sade. Certainly books can foul the atmosphere so as to engender or support abominable and criminal acts.

Finally, "prurient" depiction of sex, it is feared, may make it hard, even impossible, to control the cravings it arouses; these are felt by many persons as threats to what personality integration and Ego dominance they have achieved. It matters not at all whether the loss of control would actually occur. What matters is that the fear of losing control does. (It is often projected on others: the fearful person may see them as uncontrolled, himself as victim.) This felt threat arouses enough anxiety in many people to value censorship. Censorship thus functions as the social analogue to (and support of) individual repression. Neither would occur, did it not have necessary psychological functions, which do not become unnecessary if we demonstrate rationally that they are.

To be sure, neither repression nor censorship are ideal solutions to the problem of anxiety. But we do not live in an ideal world with ideal people. And "solutions" that ignore (or define away) the problems actual people have in the actual world are not helpful. They may make matters worse: the elimination of legal censorship would probably provoke arbitrary and damaging nonlegal censorship by private persons and groups.

"Very well," a lawyer may argue, "suppose you have shown that censorship is necessary and useful to society; and that it helps individuals yearning for pornography as well as others who want to be screened from it. But how do you determine what is to be censored? 'Lewdness' and 'prurience' are matters of opinion; so, therefore, is censorship. Because the power of the censor cannot but be used arbitrarily, by relying on one opinion or another, it endangers the freedom of literature, ultimately of all expression, no less than the license of pornography. Isn't this too high a price to pay?"

I don't think we have to pay this price. And, I know of no historical instance where censorship of pornography has endangered freedom in other areas. (The converse does occur, but is irrelevant: communism or nazism restricts freedom and *thereupon* censors pornography.) Anyway, a definition of pornography which distinguishes it from literature is neither so nearly impossible a task as some lawyers make it, nor as different from other legal distinctions as they presume. And if we can distinguish pornography from literature we can censor one without restricting the other.

Several extrinsic and intrinsic qualities set pornography apart. The extrinsic qualities are: 1) the intention of the author (or painter, comedian, actor, photographer, editor—of anyone who communicates); 2) the use made of his work—the means used to advertise and sell it, the context created for it; 3) the actual effect on the consumer.

1. If pornographic intention is admitted, or proved by testimony and circumstances, there is no problem. If doubtful, intention must be tested by the intrinsic qualities of the work.

2. Regardless of the author's intent his work may be advertised or sold by stressing its (actual or putative) prurient appeal. By itself this justifies action against the seller only. Yet, although sales tactics are neither sufficient nor necessary to establish the prurient appeal of what is sold, they can be relevant: the image created by the seller may well fuse with the object of which it is an image and have effects on the consumer. Advertisers often claim they achieve this fusion. Sometimes they can—when the object lends itself to it.*

3. The actual effect on the consumer—whether "prurient interest" is, or is not, aroused—depends on the work, its presentation, and the character of the consumer. A work not intended to be pornographic may nonetheless awaken lust, or have lewd effects; and one intended to do so may fail. Censors must consult not only their own reactions but rely on testimony about probable and prevailing reactions and standards. Pornography, to be such, must be likely to have a prurient or lewd effect. But this effect alone, though necessary, is not sufficient. However, together the three extrinsic qualities certainly are. Any two of them seem quite enough.

These qualities suffice to characterize "hardcore" pornography, which is "hardcore" precisely because it has at least two of these extrinsic qualities—and not much else to confuse matters. But what about works which cannot be classified by means of their extrinsic qualities alone—where effect or intention are mixed, or doubtful? Such works can be

---

* This is certainly the burden of part of the Supreme Court decision in the Ginzburg case.

dealt with only by exploring the intrinsic qualities which make pornography pornographic.

Characteristically, pornography, while dreary and repulsive to one part of the normal (most usual) personality, is also seductive to another: it severs sex from its human context (the Id from Ego and Superego), reduces the world to orifices and organs, the action to their combinations. Sex rages in an empty world as people use each other as its anonymous bearers or vessels, bereaved of love and hate, thought and feeling, reduced to bare sensations of pain and pleasure, existing only in (and for) incessant copulations without apprehension, conflict or relationship.

The pornographic reduction of life to varieties of sex is but the spinning out of preadolescent fantasies which reject the burdens of reality and individuation, of conflict, commitment, thought, consideration and love, of regarding others as more than objects—a burden which becomes heavier and less avoidable in adolescence. Thus in fantasy a return to the pure libidinal pleasure principle is achieved—and fantasy may regress to even more infantile fears and wishes: people are literally devoured, tortured, mutilated and altogether dehumanized. (Such fantasies are acted out—e.g. in concentration camps—whenever authority fails to control, or supports, the impulses it usually helps to repress.)

So much for the content of pornography; it has one aim only: to arouse the reader's lust so that, by sharing the fantasy manufactured for him, he may attain a vicarious sexual experience. Pornography is intended to produce this experience, unlike literature, which aims at the contemplation of experience, at the revelation of its significance. Revelation too is an experience—but one which helps understand and enlarge the possibilities and complexities of the human career—whereas pornography narrows and simplifies them till they are reduced to a series of more or less sophisticated but anonymous (therefore monotonous) sensations.

It is impossible, of course, to serve pornography pure. The vicarious experience must occur through the medium of words, and be depicted in a setting that permits the suspension of disbelief. Yet aesthetic merit would be distracting and may even, in Santayana's words, "cancel lust." To avoid this, pornographers use well-worn and inconspicuous clichés and conventions which do not encumber the libidinous purpose.

These qualities are intrinsic to pornography and distinguish it from literature. I shall not try to suggest anything about works in which pornographic stretches are combined with passages of literary merit, or "redeeming social value." They are rare, and, usually, improved without the pornographic stretches—if these are truly pornographic in quality and purpose.*

Some lawyers argue that the perception of the intrinsic qualities of pornography in any work depends on literary criticism and is therefore a matter of opinion. I think it is a matter of fact; and I don't think literary criticism is a matter of opinion (except, perhaps, for standards of valuation, not of distinction: the distinction of French from the list is factual, the valuation need not be). It seems odd, though, that in a legal context serious critics often behave as though they believed criticism to be a matter of opinion. Why be a critic—and teach the stuff to college kids—if it involves no more than uttering capricious and arbitrary opinions? And if criticism cannot tell pornography from literature what can it tell us? Of course critics may disagree; so do other witnesses, including psychiatrists and handwriting experts. The decision is up to the court; the literary witnesses only have the obligation to testify truthfully as to what is or is not pornography.

Some of the critics, who claim that they cannot make the distinction, do not wish to, because they regard pornography as legitimate; others fear that censorship of pornography may be extended to literature. Whatever the merits of such

---

* *Candy* is a pornographic work as is *Fanny Hill* or *Story of O,* or de Sade. Joyce is not pornographic; neither is Edmund Wilson, nor Hubert Selby, Jr. Norman Mailer has tried hard, but has not achieved pornography.

views, they do not justify testifying that the distinction cannot be made. A witness is not entitled to deny that he saw what he did see, simply to save the accused from a punishment he dislikes. A critic who is really incapable of distinguishing pornography from literature certainly has no business being one; a critic who is capable of making the distinction has no business testifying that he is not.

Censorship is no less possible nor less needed than pornography. If we indulge pornography, and do not allow censorship to restrict it, our society at best will become ever more coarse, brutal, anxious, indifferent, de-individualized, hedonistic; at worst its ethos will disintegrate altogether.

Susan Sontag

The Pornographic Imagination

NO ONE SHOULD UNDERTAKE A DISCUSSION OF PORNOGRAPHY BE-
fore acknowledging the pornograph*ies,* of which there are at
least three; and before pledging to take them on one at a
time. A good deal is gained by treating pornography as an
item in social history quite separately from pornography as a
psychological phenomenon (according to the usual view,
symptomatic of sexual deficiency or deformity in both the
producers and the consumers). And everything is to be
gained by distinguishing from both of these another pornography—a minor but highly interesting modality or convention within the arts.

It's the last of the three pornographies that I want to focus upon. More narrowly, upon the literary genre for which, lacking a better name, I'm willing to accept (in the privacy of serious intellectual debate, not in the courts) the dubious label of pornography. By literary genre I mean a body of work belonging to literature considered as an art, and to which inherent standards of artistic excellence pertain. From the standpoint of social and psychological phenomena, all pornographic texts have the same status; they are documents. But from the standpoint of art, some of these texts may well become something else. I for one am convinced that not only do Pierre Louÿs's *Trois Filles et leur Mère*, Georges Bataille's *Histoire de l'Oeil* and *Madame Edwarda*, the pseudonymous *Story of O* and *The Image* belong to literature, but that it can be made clear why these books, all five of them, occupy a much higher rank as literature than Oscar Wilde's *Teleny* or the Earl of Rochester's *Sodom* or Apollinaire's *The Debauched Hospodar* or Cleland's *Fanny Hill*, or *Candy*. The avalanche of pornographic potboilers marketed for two centuries under and now, increasingly, over the counter no more impugns the status as literature of at least a dozen pornographic books I have read than the proliferation of books of the caliber of *The Carpetbaggers* and *Valley of the Dolls* throws into question the credentials of *Anna Karenina* and *The Great Gatsby* and *The Man Who Loved Children*. The ratio of authentic literature to trash in pornography may be somewhat lower than the ratio of novels of genuine literary merit to the entire volume of subliterary fiction produced for mass taste. But I doubt that it's any lower than, for instance, that of another somewhat shady subgenre with a few first-rate books to its credit, science fiction. (As literary forms, pornography and science fiction resemble each other in several interesting ways.) Anyway, the quantitative measure supplies a trivial standard. Relatively uncommon as they may be, there are writings which it seems reasonable to call pornographic—assuming that the stale label has any use at all—which, at the same time, cannot be refused accreditation as serious literature.

The point would seem to be obvious. Yet, apparently, that's far from being the case. At least in England and America, the reasoned scrutiny and assessment of pornography is held firmly within the limits of the discourse employed by psychologists, sociologists, historians, jurists, professional moralists, and social critics. Pornography is a malady to be diagnosed and an occasion for judgment. It's something one is for or against. And taking sides about pornography is hardly like being for or against aleatoric music or Pop Art, but quite a bit like being for or against legalized abortion or federal aid to parochial schools. In fact, the same fundamental approach to the subject is shared by recent eloquent defenders of society's right and obligation to censor dirty books, like George P. Elliott and George Steiner,* and writers, like Paul Goodman,† who warn of pernicious consequences of a policy of censorship far worse than any harm done by the books themselves. Both the libertarians and the would-be censors agree in reducing pornography to pathological symptom and problematic social commodity. A near unanimous consensus exists as to what pornography is— this being identified with notions about the *sources* of the impulse to produce and consume these curious goods. As a theme for psychological analysis, pornography is rarely seen as anything more interesting than texts which illustrate a deplorable arrest in normal adult sexual development. On this view, all pornography amounts to is the representation of the fantasies of infantile sexual life, these fantasies having been edited by the more skilled, less innocent consciousness of the masturbatory adolescent, for purchase by so-called adults. As a social phenomenon—for instance, the boom in the production of pornography in the societies of Western Europe and America since the eighteenth century—the approach is no less unequivocally clinical. Pornography becomes a group pathology, the disease of a whole culture, about whose cause everyone is pretty well agreed. The

* See pp. 72–95 and 96–108.
† See pp. 42–60.

mounting output of dirty books is attributed to a festering legacy of Christianity-sponsored sexual repression and to sheer physiological ignorance, these ancient disabilities being now compounded by more proximate historical events, the impact of drastic dislocations in traditional modes of family and political order and unsettling change in the roles of the sexes. (The problem of pornography is one of "the dilemmas of a society in transition," Goodman said in an essay several years ago.) * Thus, there is a fairly complete consensus about the *diagnosis* of pornography itself. The disagreements arise only in the estimate of the psychological and social *consequences* of its dissemination, and therefore in the formulating of tactics and policy.

The more enlightened architects of moral policy are undoubtedly prepared to admit that there is something like a "pornographic imagination"; although only in the sense that pornographic works are tokens of a radical failure or deformation of the imagination. And they may grant, as Goodman, Wayland Young, and others have suggested, that there also exists a "pornographic society": that, indeed, ours is a flourishing example of one, a society so hypocritically and repressively constructed that it must inevitably produce an effusion of pornography as both its logical expression and its subversive, demotic antidote. But nowhere in the Anglo-American community of letters have I seen it argued that some pornographic books are interesting and important works of art. So long as pornography is treated as only a social and psychological phenomenon and a locus for moral concern, how could such an argument ever be made?

II

There's another reason, apart from this presumption about what pornography is as a topic of analysis, why the question of whether or not works of pornography can be literature has never been genuinely debated. I mean the view of litera-

* See pp. 42–60.

ture itself maintained by most English and American critics —a view which in excluding pornographic writings *by definition* from the precincts of literature excludes much else besides.

Of course, no one denies that pornography constitutes a branch of literature in the sense that it can take the form of printed books of fiction. But beyond that trivial correspondence, no more is allowed. The way most critics construe the "nature" of prose literature, no less than their view of the "nature" of pornography, must put pornography in an adverse relation to literature. A pornographic book is defined as one not belonging to literature (and vice versa), which suggests there's no need to examine the books.

One common charge is that the utterly singleminded way in which works of pornography address the reader, proposing to arouse him sexually, is antithetical to the complex function of literature. It may then be argued that pornography's aim, that of inducing sexual excitement, is at odds with the tranquil, detached involvement evoked by genuine art. But this seems particularly unconvincing, in view of the much admired appeal to the reader's moral feelings that "realistic" writing generally intends. It's more plausible to emphasize just the very singleness of pornography's aim, while acknowledging that some certified masterpieces (from Chaucer to Lawrence) do properly excite readers sexually in certain passages or sections. Nevertheless, the argument goes, pornography still possesses only one "intention," while any genuinely valuable work of literature has many.

Another common argument, offered by Adorno among others, is that works of pornography lack the beginning-middle-and-end form characteristic of literature. A piece of pornographic fiction concocts no better than a crude excuse for a beginning; and once having begun, it goes on and on and ends nowhere.

Another argument is that pornographic writing can't evidence any care for its means of expression as such (the concern of literature), since the aim of pornography is to inspire a set of nonverbal fantasies in which language plays a debased, merely instrumental role.

Last and most weighty is the following argument. The subject of literature is something called "the human," that is, the relation of human beings to each other, their complex feelings and emotions; pornography, in contrast, disdains fully formed persons (psychology and social portrayal), is oblivious to the question of motives and their credibility, and reports only the motiveless tireless transactions of depersonalized organs. Simply extrapolating from the conception of what a work of literature is maintained by most English and American critics writing today, it would follow that the literary value of pornography has to be nil.

But this argument by paradigm simply won't do. Even taking the prevailing concept of literature and applying it to, say, *Story of O,* there's scarcely a single respect in which it fits. Though the novel is thoroughly obscene by the usual standards, and more effective than many in arousing a reader sexually, it can't be said that sexual arousal is the sole function of the situations portrayed. The narrative does have a definite beginning, middle, and end. Far from giving the impression that its author considered language a bothersome necessity, the book is written in an elegant, accomplished French (whose quality the translation doesn't put over too well into English). Further, the characters do possess emotions of a very intense kind, although obsessional and indeed wholly asocial ones; characters do have motives, though they are not psychiatrically or socially "normal" motives. The characters in *Story of O* are endowed with a "psychology" of a sort, one derived from the psychology of lust. And while what is learned of the characters within the situations in which they are placed is severely restricted—to modes of sexual concentration and explicitly rendered sexual behavior—O and her partners are, in form, no more reduced or foreshortened than the characters in many nonpornographic works of contemporary fiction.

The fact is, if English and American critics had a more sophisticated view of literature, an interesting debate could get under way. (In the end, this debate would be not only about pornography, but about the whole body of contemporary literature insistently focused on extreme situations and behavior.) The difficulty is that so many critics continue to identify with prose literature itself the particular literary conventions of "realism" (what might be crudely associated with the major tradition of the nineteenth-century novel). For examples of alternative literary modes, one is not confined to appealing only to much of the greatest twentieth-century writing—to *Ulysses,* which is a book not about characters but about media of transpersonal exchange, about all that's outside individual psychology and personal need, to French Surrealism and its most recent offspring, the New Novel, to German "expressionist" fiction, to the Russian post-novel represented by Biely's *St. Petersburg* and by Nabokov, or to the nonlinear tenseless narratives of Stein and Burroughs. A definition of literature that faults a work for being rooted in "fantasy" rather than in the realistic rendering of how life-like persons in familiar situations live with each other couldn't even handle such venerable conventions as the pastoral, which depicts relations between people that could scarcely be more reductive, vapid, or unconvincing.

An uprooting of some of these tenacious clichés is long overdue: it will promote a sounder reading of the literature of the past as well as put critics and ordinary readers better in touch with contemporary literature, which includes zones of writing that structurally resemble pornography. It's too easy, virtually meaningless, to demand that literature stick with the "human." For what is at stake is not "human" versus "inhuman" (in which choosing the "human" guarantees instant moral self-congratulation for both author and reader) but an infinitely varied register of forms and tonalities for transposing *the human voice* into prose narrative. From the point of view of criticism, the proper question is not the relationship between the book and "the world" or "reality" (in which each book of fiction is judged as if it were a unique item, and in which the world is taken as a far less complex place than it is) but the complexities of consciousness itself, as the medium through which "a world" exists at all and is constituted, and an approach to single books which doesn't slight the way they exist in dialogue with each other. From this point of view, the decision of the old novelists to depict the unfolding of the destinies of sharply individualized "characters" in familiar, socially dense situations within the conventional notation of chronological sequence is only one of many possible decisions, with no inherently superior claim to the allegiance of serious readers. There is nothing innately more "human" about these procedures of the old novelists. The presence of realistic "characters" isn't, in itself, something wholesome. Nor is it more nourishing for the moral sensibility.

The only sure thing that can be said about characters in prose fiction is that they are, to use the phrase of Henry James, "a compositional resource." The presence of human figures in literary art can serve many purposes. Dramatic tension or three-dimensionality in the rendering of personal and social relations is often *not* what is being aimed at, in which case it doesn't help to insist on that as a generic standard. The presentation of lifelike persons is far from being a necessary staple of literature. The exploration of ideas is as authentic an aim of prose fiction, although the adoption of this aim severely limits the representation of persons by the standards of novelistic realism. The constructing or imaging of something inanimate, or of part of the world of nature, is also a valid enterprise, and entails an appropriate rescaling of the human figure. (The form of the pastoral involves a mixture of both these aims: the depiction of ideas and of nature. Persons are used only to the extent that they create a certain kind of landscape, which is partly a stylization of "real" nature and partly a neo-Platonic landscape of ideas.) And equally valid as a subject for prose narrative are the extreme states of human feeling and consciousness, those so peremptory that they exclude the mundane flux of feelings and are only contingently linked with concrete persons—which is the case with pornography.

One would never know, from the confident generalizations on the "nature" of literature set forth by most American and English critics, that a stirring debate on the issue had been going on now for several generations. As Jacques Rivière wrote in the *NRF* in 1924, "It seems to me that we are witnessing a very serious crisis in the concept of what literature is." One of several responses to "the problem of the possibility and the limits of literature," Rivière notes, is the marked tendency for "art (if even the word can still be kept) to become a completely nonhuman activity, a supersensory function, if I may use the term, a sort of creative astronomy." I have cited Rivière not because his essay, "Questioning the Concept of Literature," is particularly original or definitive or subtly argued, but merely to recall to mind that group of radical notions about literature, which were almost critical commonplaces forty years ago in European magazines comparable to *Partisan Review*.

To this day, though, that ferment remains something alien, unassimilated, and persistently misunderstood in the English and American world of letters: suspected as issuing from a collective cultural failure of nerve, frequently dismissed as outright perversity or obscurantism or creative sterility. The better English-speaking critics could, however, hardly fail to notice how much great twentieth-century literature subverts those ideas received from certain of the great nineteenth-century novelists on the "nature" of literature which they continue to echo in 1967. But the critics' awareness of genuinely new literature was usually tendered in a spirit much like that of the rabbis a century before the beginning of the Christian era who, humbly acknowledging the spiritual inferiority of their own age to the age of the great prophets, nevertheless firmly closed the canon of prophetic books and declared—with more relief, one suspects, than regret—the era of prophecy ended. So was the age of what in Anglo-American criticism is still called, aston-

ishingly enough, "experimental" or "avant-garde" writing repeatedly declared to be closed. The ritual celebration of
each contemporary genius's undermining of the older notions of literature was often accompanied by the nervous in-
sistence that the writing brought forth was, alas, the last of
its noble, sterile line. Now, the results of this intricate one-
eyed way of looking at modern literature have been several
decades of unparalleled interest and brilliance in English
and American—particularly American—criticism. But it
is an interest and brilliance that's reared on bankruptcy of
taste and something approaching a fundamental dishonesty
of method. The critics' retrograde awareness of the impressive new claims staked out by modern literature, linked with
their chagrin over what was usually designated as "the rejection of reality" and "the failure of the self" endemic in that
literature, indicates the precise point at which most talented
Anglo-American literary criticism leaves off considering
structures of literature and transposes itself into criticism of
culture.

I don't wish to repeat here the arguments that I have advanced elsewhere on behalf of a different critical approach.
Still, some allusion to that approach needs to be made. To
discuss even a single work of the radical nature of *Histoire
de l'Oeil* raises the question of literature itself, of prose narrative considered as an art form. Books like those of Bataille
could not have been written except for that intellectual up-
heaval over the nature of literature which has been taking
place in Europe for more than half a century; but lacking
that context, they must be almost unassimilable for English
and American readers—except as "mere" pornography,
mysteriously fancy trash. If it is even necessary to take up the
issue of whether or not pornography and literature are antithetical, if it is at all necessary to assert that works of pornography *can* belong to literature, then the assertion has to
imply an over-all view of what art is.

To put the matter most generally: art (and art-making) is
a form of consciousness; the materials of art are the variety

of forms of consciousness. And no *esthetic* principle exists by which this notion of the materials of art can be construed as excluding even the most extreme forms of consciousness that transcend social personality or psychological individuality.

In daily life, to be sure, we may acknowledge a moral obligation to inhibit such states of consciousness in ourselves. The obligation seems pragmatically sound. Such inhibition on the part of most seems necessary for social order in the widest sense, and seems necessary on the part of each in order to establish and maintain a humane contact with other persons (though that contact can be renounced, for shorter or longer periods). It's well known that when people venture into the extremities of consciousness, they do so at the peril of their sanity, that is to say, of their humanity. But the "human-scale" or humanistic standard proper to ordinary life and conduct seems misplaced when applied to art. It oversimplifies. If within the last century art conceived as an autonomous activity has come to be invested with an unprecedented stature—the nearest thing to a sacramental human activity acknowledged by a secular society—it is because one of the things art has elected to do is to make forays into and take up positions on the frontiers of consciousness (often very dangerous to the artist as a person) and to report back what's there. Being a free-lance explorer of spiritual dangers, the artist is given a certain license to behave differently from other people; matching the singularity of his vocation, he may or may not be decked out with a suitably eccentric life style. But his main job is to invent trophies of his experiences—objects and gestures that fascinate and enthrall, not merely (as older notions of the artist would have it) edify or entertain. His principal means of fascinating is to advance one step further in the dialectic of outrage. To make his work repulsive, obscure, inaccessible; in short, to give what is, or seems to be, *not* wanted. But however fierce may be the outrages he perpetrates upon his audience, the artist's credentials and spiritual authority ultimately depend

on the audience's sense (whether something known or in-
ferred) of the outrages he commits upon himself. The exemplary modern artist is a broker in madness.

The notion of art as the dearly purchased fruits of an immense spiritual risk, one whose cost goes up with the entry
and participation of each new player in the game, invites a
new set of critical standards. Certainly, the art produced
under the aegis of this conception is not, cannot be, "realistic." But words that merely invert the guidelines of realism
—like "fantasy" or "surrealism"—don't clarify much.
Fantasy all too easily declines into "mere" fantasy; the
clincher is the adjective "infantile." Where does fantasy, condemned by psychiatric rather than artistic standards, end
and imagination begin?

Since it's hardly likely that most contemporary critics seriously mean to bar prose narratives that are unrealistic from
the domain of literature, one suspects that a special standard
is being applied to sexual themes. Transfer to another kind
of book, another kind of "fantasy," and the matter becomes
clear. The ahistorical dreamlike landscape in which action is
situated, the peculiarly congealed time in which acts are
performed—these occur almost as often in science fiction
as they do in pornography. There is nothing very remarkable in the fact that most men and women fall short of the
sexual prowess people in pornography are represented as enjoying; that size of organs, number and duration of orgasms,
variety and feasibility of sexual postures, and amount of sexual energy available all seem grossly exaggerated. Yes, and
the spaceships and the teeming planets depicted in science-
fiction novels don't exist either. That the site of narrative is
an ideal *topos* doesn't disqualify either pornography or science fiction from being literature. Such negations of real,
concrete, three-dimensional social time, space, and
personality—and such "fantastic" enlargements of human
energy—are rather the ingredients of another kind of literature, founded on another mode of consciousness.

The materials that go into the pornographic books which

count as a branch of literature are, precisely, one of the extreme forms of human consciousness. Of course, many people would agree that the sexually obsessed consciousness can, in principle, enter into literature considered as an art form. Literature about lust? Why not? But then they usually add a rider to the agreement which effectually nullifies it. What's asked is that the author of such a work have the proper "distance" from his obsessions for their rendering to count as literature. This is a hypocritical standard, revealing once again that the values most people employ to deal with pornography are, in the end, those belonging to psychiatry and social affairs rather than to art. (Since Christianity upped the ante and concentrated on sexual behavior as the core of virtue, everything pertaining to sex has been a "special case" in our culture, evoking peculiarly inconsistent attitudes.) Van Gogh's paintings are not considered less admirable nor does their status as art become dubious because there is reason to think that his manner of painting had less to do with a conscious choice of representational means, according to esthetic or art-history standards, than with the fact that he was deranged and actually saw reality the way he painted. Similarly, *Histoire de l'Oeil* does not become case history rather than art because the extraordinary autobiographical essay appended to the narrative reveals that these obscene obsessions are indeed Bataille's own.

What makes a work of pornography part of the history of art rather than of trash is not distance, the superimposition of a consciousness more conformable to that of ordinary reality upon the "deranged consciousness" of the erotically obsessed. It is rather the originality, thoroughness, authenticity, and power of that "deranged consciousness" itself, as it is incarnated in a work. From the point of view of art, the exclusivity of the consciousness embodied in pornographic books is, in itself, neither anomalous nor antiliterary.

Nor is its purported aim or effect (whether it is intentional or not)—to excite the reader sexually—a defect. Only by following a degraded and mechanistic idea of sex could one be mislead into thinking that to be sexually stirred by a book like *Madame Edwarda* is a simple matter. That singleness of intention often condemned by critics is, when the work of pornography merits treatment as art, compounded of many resonances. The physical sensations involuntarily produced in the reader carry with them something that touches upon the reader's whole experience of his humanity—and his limits as a personality and as a body. Actually, the singleness of pornography's intention is spurious. But the aggressiveness of the intention is not. What seems in pornography like an end is as much a means, startlingly and oppressively concrete. The end, though, is less concrete. Pornography is one of the branches of literature—science fiction is another—aiming at disorientation, at psychic dislocation.

In some respects, the use of sexual obsessions as a subject for literature resembles that of a subject whose validity far fewer people would contest: religious obsessions. So compared, the familiar fact of pornography's definite, aggressive impact upon its readers looks somewhat different. Its celebrated intention of sexually stimulating readers is really a species of proselytizing. Pornography that is serious literature aims to "excite" in the same way that books which render an extreme form of religious experience aim to "convert."

III

Two French books recently translated into English, *Story of O* and *The Image*, conveniently illustrate some issues involved in the topic, barely explored in Anglo-American criticism, of pornography as a branch of serious literature.

Story of O by "Pauline Réage" was published in Paris in 1954, and immediately became famous, partly due to the patronage of Jean Paulhan, who wrote the preface. It was widely believed that Paulhan had written the book, too—perhaps because of the precedent set by Bataille, who had contributed an essay (signed with his own name) to his *Madame Edwarda* when it was first published in 1941 under the pseudonym "Pierre Angelique," and also because Pauline suggested Paulhan. But Paulhan has always denied that he wrote *Story of O*, insisting that it was indeed by a woman, someone living in another part of France who didn't wish her name known. Though Paulhan's story about the unambitious provincial author was not generally believed, the conviction that it was he who wrote the book eventually faded. In the years since, a number of more ingenious hypotheses, attributing the book's authorship to other figures on the Paris literary scene, gained credence; and then were dropped. The real identity of "Pauline Réage" remains one of the few well-kept secrets in contemporary letters.

The Image came out two years later, in 1956, also under a pseudonym, "Jean de Berg," and, to compound the mystery, dedicated to and with a preface by "Pauline Réage," who has not been heard from since. (The preface by "Réage" is terse and forgettable; the one by Paulhan is long and very interesting.) Speculation at Paris literary parties about the identity of "Jean de Berg" is at least more restful than the gossip about "Pauline Réage." One rumor only, which names the wife of an influential younger novelist, has swept the field.

It's not unreasonable that those curious enough to speculate about the real people behind the two pseudonyms should regularly come up with some name from the established community of letters in France. That either of these two books should be an amateur's stroke of genius is almost inconceivable. Both, but particularly *Story of O*, are highly "literary" books. By this I mean that, different as one is from the other, both *Story of O* and *The Image* evince a quality in the writing that can't be ascribed simply to an abundance of the usual writerly endowments of sensibility, energy, and intelligence. Such gifts were surely present, but one is also aware of the extent to which these gifts have themselves been processed through a dialogue of artifices. The degree of somber self-consciousness with which the narratives are executed could hardly be farther from the lack of control and craft usually considered as accompanying the expression of obsessive lust. The fact is that, intoxicating as is their subject (if the reader doesn't cut off and find it just funny or sinister), both narratives have more to do with the "use" of erotic material than with the "expression" of it. And this use is pre-eminently—there is no other word for it—literary. The imagination pursuing its outrageous pleasures in *Story of O* and *The Image* is firmly anchored to certain notions of the *formal* consummation of intense feeling, of procedures for exhausting an experience, that connect as much with literature and recent literary history as with the ahistorical domain of eros. And why not? Experiences aren't pornographic; only expressions and representations—structures of the imagination—are. This is why what a pornographic book can make the reader think of, mainly, is other pornographic books, rather than sex unmediated—and this not necessarily to the detriment of his erotic excitement.

To take only one of many connections with the idea of literature as such projected by *Story of O:* what resonates throughout the book is a voluminous body of pornographic or "Libertine" literature, mostly trash, in both French and English, going back to the eighteenth century. The most obvious reference is to Sade. But here one must not think only of the writings of Sade himself, but of the reinterpretation of Sade by French literary intellectuals after World War II, a critical gesture perhaps comparable in its importance and influence upon educated literary taste and upon the actual direction of serious fiction in France to the reappraisal of James launched just before World War II in the United States, except that the French reappraisal has lasted longer and seems to have struck deeper roots. (Sade, of course, had never been forgotten. He was read enthusiastically by Flaubert, Baudelaire, and most of the other radical geniuses of French literature of the second half of the nineteenth century. He was one of the patron saints of the Surrealist movement, and figures importantly in the thought of Breton. But it was the writings after 1945 that really consolidated Sade's position as an inexhaustible point of departure for radical thinking about the possibilities of the human condition. The well-known essay of Beauvoir, the indefatigable scholarly biography undertaken by Gilbert Lely, and writings as yet untranslated by Blanchot, Paulhan, Bataille, Klossowski, and Leiris constitute the most eminent documents of the postwar re-evaluation which secured this astonishingly hardy modification of French literary sensibility. The quality and theoretical density of the French interest in Sade remains virtually incomprehensible to English and American literary intellectuals, for whom Sade is perhaps an exemplary figure in the history of psychopathology, both individual and social, but inconceivable as someone to be taken seriously, in an ahistorical context, as a "thinker.")

But it's not only Sade, and both the problems he raised and the ones raised in his name, that stands behind *Story of O*. There are also the conventions of the "libertine" potboilers written in nineteenth-century France, such as those which take place in a fantasy England populated by brutal aristocrats with enormous sexual equipment and violent tastes, along the axis of sadomasochism, to match. The name of O's second lover-proprietor, Sir Stephen, is clearly a reference, a kind of homage, to this highly period fantasy, as is the Sir Edmond of *Histoire de l'Oeil*. What's important to note is that the allusion to a stock type of pornographic trash stands, as a literary reference, on exactly the same footing as the anachronistic setting of most of the action, which is lifted straight from Sade's books. The narrative opens in Paris with O joining her lover René in a car and driving around, but most of the subsequent action is removed to more familiar if less plausible territory: that conveniently isolated château, luxuriously furnished and lavishly staffed with servants, where a group of rich men congregate and to which women are brought as virtual slaves in order to be the objects, shared in common, of the men's brutal and inventive lust. There are whips and chains, masks worn by the men when the women are admitted to their presence, great fires burning in the hearth, unspeakable sexual indignities, floggings and more ingenious kinds of physical mutilation, several lesbian scenes when the excitement of the orgies in the great drawing room seem to flag. In short, the novel comes equipped with some of the creakiest items in the repertoire of pornography.

How seriously are we to take this? A bare inventory of the plot might give the impression that *Story of O* is not so much pornography as metapornography, a brilliant parody. Something similar was urged in defense of *Candy* when it was published here several years ago, after some years of more modest existence in Paris as a more or less official dirty book. *Candy* wasn't pornography, it was argued, but a spoof, a witty burlesque of the conventions of cheap pornographic narrative. A good try, but it isn't so. *Candy* may be funny, but it's still pornography. For pornography isn't a form which can parody itself. It is the nature of the pornographic imagination to prefer readymade conventions of character, setting and action. Pornography is a theater of types, never of individuals. A parody of pornography always remains pornography (so far as it's at all competent). Indeed, parody is one common form of pornographic writing. Sade himself often used it, inverting the moralistic fictions of Richardson in which female virtue always triumphs over male lewdness, either by saying no or by dying afterwards. With *Story of O,* it would be more accurate to speak of a "use" rather than of a parody of Sade.

The tone alone of *Story of O* indicates that whatever in the book might be read as parody or antiquarianism—a mandarin pornography?—is only one of several elements forming the narrative. (Although sexual situations encompassing all the expectable variations of lust are graphically described, the prose style is rather formal, the level of language dignified and almost chaste.) Features of the Sadean staging are used to shape the action, but the narrative's basic line differs fundamentally from anything Sade wrote. Consider his *120 Days of Sodom,* probably the most ambitious pornographic book ever conceived (in terms of scale), a kind of summa of the pornographic imagination; stunningly impressive and upsetting, even in the truncated form, part narrative and part scenario, in which it has survived. (The manuscript was accidentally rescued from the Bastille after Sade had been forced to leave it behind when he was transferred in 1789 to Charenton, but Sade believed until his death that his masterpiece had been destroyed when the prison was razed.) Sade's express train of outrages tears along an interminable but level track. His descriptions are too schematic to be sensuous. The actions of the book are illustrations, rather, of his relentlessly repeated ideas. Yet these polemical ideas themselves seem, eventually, more like principles of a dramaturgy than a serious theory. Sade's ideas—of the person as a "thing" or an "object," of the body as a machine, and of the orgy as an inventory of the hopefully indefinite possibilities of several machines in collaboration with each other—seems mainly designed to make possible an endless, nonculminating kind of ultimately affectless activity. In contrast, there is a definite movement in *Story of O;* a logic of events, as opposed to Sade's static principle of the catalogue or encyclopedia. This plot movement is certainly abetted by the fact that, for most of the narrative, the author tolerates at least a vestige of the unit of "the couple" (O and René, O and Sir Stephen)—a unit generally repudiated in pornographic literature.

And, of course, the figure of O herself is different. Her feelings, however insistently they adhere to one theme, have some modulation and are carefully described. If O is passive, she is scarcely like those ninnies in Sade's tales who are detained in remote castles to be tormented by cliques of pitiless noblemen and satanic priests. And O is represented as active, too; literally active, as in the seduction of Jacqueline, and more important, profoundly active in her own passivity. Only superficially does O resemble her predecessors in Sade's writings. There is never any personal consciousness, except that of the author, in Sade's books. But O does possess a consciousness, from which vantage point her story is told. (Although written in the third person, the narrative never departs from O's point of view or understands more than she understands.) Sade's effort is to neutralize sexuality of all its personal associations, to represent a kind of impersonal— or pure—sexual encounter. But the narrative of "Pauline Réage" does show O reacting in quite different ways (including love) to different people, notably to René, to Sir Stephen, to Jacqueline, and to Anne-Marie.

Sade, of course, is more representative of the major conventions of pornographic writing. So far as the pornographic imagination tends to make one person interchangeable with another and all people interchangeable with things, it's not functional to describe a person as O is described—in terms of a certain state of her will (which she's trying to discard) and of her understanding. Pornography is mainly populated by creatures like Sade's Justine, endowed with neither will, intelligence, nor even, apparently, memory. Justine lives in a perpetual state of astonishment, never learning anything from the strikingly repetitious violations of her innocence. After each fresh betrayal she gets in place for another round, as uninstructed by her experience as ever, ready to trust the next masterful libertine and be rewarded for it by a renewed loss of liberty, the same indignities, and the same blasphemous sermons in praise of vice.

For the most part, the figures who play the role of sexual objects in pornography are made of the same stuff as a principal "humour" of comedy. Justine is like Candide, who is also a cipher, a blank, an eternal naïf who can learn nothing from his atrocious ordeals. The familiar structure of comedy which features a character who is a kind of still center in the midst of outrage (Buster Keaton is a classic image) crops up repeatedly in pornography. The personages in pornography, like those of comedy, are seen only from the outside, behavioristically. By definition, they can't be seen in depth, so as truly to engage the audience's feelings. In much of comedy, the joke resides precisely in the *disparity* between the understated or anesthetized feeling and a large outrageous event. Pornography works in a similar fashion. What's gained by a deadpan tone, by what seems to the reader in an ordinary state of consciousness to be the incredible *under*reacting of most of the characters to the situations in which they're placed, isn't the release of laughter. It's the release of a sexual reaction, originally voyeuristic but probably needing to be secured by an underlying direct identification with one of the participants in the sexual act. The emotional flatness of pornography is thus neither a failure of artistry nor an index of principled inhumanity. The arousal of a sexual response in the reader *requires* it. Only in the absence of directly stated emotions is the reader of pornography likely to have room for his own responses. When the event narrated comes already festooned with the author's explicitly avowed sentiments, the reader may be stirred by those sentiments. But it's harder to be stirred by the event itself.*

Silent film comedy offers many illustrations of how the formal principle of continual agitation or perpetual motion (slapstick) and that of the deadpan really amount to the same thing—a deadening or neutralization or distancing of the audience's emotions, its ability to identify in a "humane" way and to bring moral judgments (etc.) about situations of violence. The same principle is at work in all pornography. It's not that the characters in pornography cannot conceivably possess any emotions. They can. Still, the principles of underreacting and frenetic agitation make the emo-

---

* This is very clear in the case of Genet's books which, despite the explicitness of the sexual experiences related, are not sexually arousing for most readers. What the reader knows (and Genet has stated it many times) is that Genet himself was sexually excited while writing *The Miracle of the Rose, Our Lady of the Flowers*, etc. The reader makes an intense and unsettling contact with Genet's erotic excitement, which is the energy that propels these metaphor-studded narratives; but, at the same time, the author's excitement precludes the reader's own. Genet was perfectly correct when he said that his books were not pornographic.

tional climate self-canceling, so that the basic tone of pornography is affectless, emotionless.

However, degrees of this affectlessness can be distinguished. Justine is the stereotype sex-object figure (invariably female, since most pornography is written by men or from the stereotyped male point of view): a bewildered victim, whose consciousness, as I have said, is never changed in the slightest by her experiences. But O is an adept; grateful, whatever the cost in pain and fear, for the opportunity to be initiated into a mystery. That mystery is the loss of the self. O learns, she suffers, she changes. Step by step she becomes more what she is, a process identical with the emptying out of herself. In the vision of the world presented by *Story of O,* the highest good is the transcendence of personality. The plot's movement is not horizontal, but a kind of ascent through degradation. O does not simply become identical with her sexual availability, but wants to reach the perfection of becoming an "object." Her condition, if it can be characterized as one of "dehumanization," is not to be understood as a by-product of her situation of enslavement to René, Sir Stephen, and the other men at Roissy. It's exactly the point of her situation, something she seeks and eventually attains. Her achievement is represented in the last scene of the book when she's led to a party, mutilated, in chains, unrecognizable, costumed (as an owl)—so convincingly no longer human that none of the guests even thinks of speaking to her directly.

O's quest is neatly summed up in the expressive letter which serves her for a name. "O" suggests a cartoon of her sex, not her individual sex but simply woman; it also stands for the void, a vacuity, a nothing. But what *Story of O* unfolds is a spiritual paradox, that of the full void and of the vacuity that is also a plenum. The power of the book lies exactly in the anguish stirred up by the continuing presence of this paradox. "Pauline Réage" raises, in a far more organic and sophisticated manner than Sade does with his clumsy expositions and discourses, the question of the status of human personality itself. But whereas Sade is interested in the obliteration of personality from the viewpoint of power and liberty, the author of *Story of O* is interested in the obliteration of personality from the viewpoint of happiness. (The closest thing to a statement of this theme we possess in English literature are certain passages in Lawrence's *The Lost Girl*.)

For the paradox to gain real significance, however, depends on at least glimpsing a view of sex different from that held by most enlightened members of the community. The prevailing view—an amalgam of Rousseauist, Freudian, and liberal social thought—estimates the phenomenon of sex as a perfectly intelligible although uniquely precious source of emotional and physical pleasure. What difficulties there are come from the long deformation of the sexual impulses administered by Western Christianity, whose ugly wounds scarcely anyone in this culture escapes. First, guilt and anxiety. Then, the reduction of sexual capacities leading if not to virtual impotence or frigidity, at least to the depletion of erotic energy and the repression of many natural elements of sexual appetite (the "perversions"). Then the spillover into public dishonesties in which people tend to respond to news of the sexual pleasures of others with envy, fascination, revulsion, and spiteful indignation. It's from this pollution of the sexual health of the culture that a phenomenon like pornography is derived.

Now, what's decisive in the complex of views held by most educated members of the community is the assumption that human sexual appetite is, if untampered with, a natural pleasant function; and that "the obscene" is a convention, the fiction imposed upon nature by a society convinced that there is something vile about the sexual functions, and by extension, about sexual pleasure. It's just these assumptions that are challenged by the French tradition represented by Sade, Lautréamont, Bataille, and the authors of *Story of O* and *The Image*. Their assumption seems to be that "the obscene" is a primal notion of human consciousness, something much more profound than the backwash of a sick society's aversion to the body. Human sexuality is, quite apart from Christian repressions, etc., a highly questionable phenomenon, and belongs, at least potentially, among the extreme rather than the ordinary experiences of humanity. Tamed as it may be, sexuality remains one of the demonic forces in human consciousness—pushing us at intervals close to taboo and dangerous desires, which range from the impulse to commit sudden arbitrary violence upon another person to the voluptuous yearning for the extinction of one's consciousness, for death itself. Even on the level of simple physical sensation and mood, making love surely resembles having an epileptic fit at least as much as, if not more than, it does eating a meal or conversing with someone. Everyone has felt (at least in fantasy) the erotic glamor of physical cruelty and an erotic lure in things which are vile and repulsive. These phenomena are part of the genuine spectrum of sexuality, and if they are not to be written off as mere neurotic aberrations, the picture may look different from the one promoted by enlightened public opinion, and less simple.

It almost seems as if it's for good reason that most people's whole capacity for sexual ecstasy is inaccessible to them, given that each person's sexuality is something, like nuclear energy, that may prove amenable to domestication through scruple, but then again, it may not. That most people do not regularly, or perhaps ever, experience their sexual capacities at this unsettling pitch doesn't mean that the extreme isn't authentic, or that the possibility of it doesn't haunt them anyway. (Religion is probably, after sex, the second oldest resource which human beings have available to them for blowing their minds. Yet among the multitudes of the pious, the number who have ventured very far with that state of consciousness must be fairly small, too.) There is, demonstrably, something incorrectly designed and potentially disorienting in the human sexual capacity—at least in the capacities of man-in-civilization. Man, the sick animal, bears within him an appetite which can drive him mad. And it's that understanding of sexuality as something beyond good and evil, beyond love, beyond sanity, sexuality as a resource for ordeal and for breaking through limits of consciousness, that informs the French books which I've been talking about.

Story of O, with its project for completely transcending the idea of personality, rests on this dark and complex vision of sexuality—so far removed from the hopeful view sponsored by American Freudianism and liberal culture. The woman who is given no other name than "O" progresses simultaneously toward her own extinction as a human being and her fulfillment as a sexual being. It's hard to know how anyone would ascertain whether there is truly anything in "nature" or human consciousness that supports such a split. But, surely, the possibility has always haunted man, as accustomed as he is to decrying such a split.

O's project enacts, on another scale, no more than what's performed by the existence of pornographic literature itself. What pornographic literature does is precisely to drive a wedge between one's existence as a full human being and one's existence as a sexual being—while in ordinary life one hopes to prevent such a wedge from being driven. Normally we don't experience, at least don't want to experience, our sexual fulfillment as distinct from or opposed to our personal fulfillment. But perhaps in part they are distinct, whether we like it or not. Insofar as strong sexual feeling does involve an obsessive degree of attention, it surely does contain experiences in which one can feel one is losing one's "self." The literature that goes from Sade through Surrealism to these more recent books precisely capitalizes on that mystery, isolates that and makes the reader aware of it, invites him to participate in it.

This literature is both an invocation of the erotic in its darkest sense and, in certain cases, an exorcism. The devout, solemn mood of *Story of O* is fairly unrelieved; an example of a work of mixed moods on the same theme of a journey toward the estrangement of the self from the self is Buñuel's film *L'Age d'Or*. Perhaps it would be worth positing that pornography as a literary form works with both a pattern equivalent to tragedy (as in *Story of O*) in which the erotic subject-victim heads inexorably toward death and an equivalent to comedy (as in *The Image*) in which the obsessional pursuit of sexual exercise is rewarded by a terminal gratification, union with the uniquely desired sexual partner.

IV

Bataille is the writer who works with a darker sense of the erotic, its perils of fascination and humiliation, than probably anyone. His *Histoire de l'Oeil* (first published in 1921) and *Madame Edwarda* (1941),* qualify as pornographic books so far as their theme is sexual quest, an all-engrossing quest which annihilates every consideration of persons extraneous to their roles in the sexual dramaturgy, and the fulfillment of this quest is depicted graphically. But this conveys nothing of their extraordinary quality. For sheer explicitness about sexual organs and acts is in no sense necessarily obscene; it only becomes so when delivered in a particular tone, when it has acquired a certain moral resonance. As it happens, the sparse number of sexual acts and quasi-sexual defilements related in Bataille's novellas can hardly compete, either in number or variety, with the interminable mechanistic inventiveness of *120 Days of Sodom*. Yet what he describes seems somehow more potent and outrageous than the most lurid orgies that Sade could stage, because Bataille possessed a much finer and more profound sense of transgression.

One reason that *Histoire de l'Oeil* and *Madame Edwarda* make such an extreme and upsetting impression is that Bataille understood more clearly than anyone else that what

---

* It's unfortunate that the only translation available in this country of what purports to be *Madame Edwarda*, that included in *The Olympia Reader*, pp. 662–673, published by Grove Press two years ago, gives just half the work. Only the *récit* is translated. But *Madame Edwarda* isn't a *récit* padded out with a preface also by Bataille. It is a two-part invention—essay and *récit* —and one part is almost unintelligible without the other.

pornography is really about, ultimately, isn't sex, but death. This is not to suggest that every pornographic work speaks, either overtly or covertly, of death. Only those works which deal with that specific and strongest inflection of the themes of lust, "the obscene," do. It's toward the gratifications of death, succeeding and surpassing those of eros, that every truly obscene quest tends. (An example of a pornographic work that isn't about the "obscene" is Louÿs's jolly saga of sexual insatiability, *Trois Filles et leur Mère. The Image* presents a less clear-cut case. While the enigmatic transactions between the three characters are charged with a sense of the obscene—more like a premonition, since the obscene is reduced to being only a constituent of voyeurism —the upshot is an unequivocally happy ending, with the narrator finally united with Claire. In *Story of O* there is another sort of problem. The book ends ambiguously, with several lines to the effect that two versions of a final suppressed chapter exist, in one of which O received Sir Stephen's permission to die when he was about to discard her. Although this double ending satisfyingly echoes the book's opening, in which two versions "of the same beginning" are given, it shouldn't, I think, shake the reader's sense that O is death-bound, whatever doubts the author expresses about her fate.)

Bataille's books, the chamber music of pornographic literature, are usually in *récit* form (sometimes accompanied by an essay). Their unifying theme is Bataille's own consciousness, a consciousness in an acute, unrelenting state of agony; but as an equally extraordinary mind in an earlier age might have written a theology of agony, Bataille has written an erotics of agony. Willing to tell something of the autobiographical sources of his narratives, he appended to *Histoire de l'Oeil* some memories of his own outrageously terrible childhood. (One memory: his blind, syphilitic, insane father trying unsuccessfully to urinate.) Time has neutralized these memories, he explains; after many years, they have largely lost their power over him and "can only come to life again, deformed, hardly recognizable, having in the course of this deformation, taken on an obscene meaning." Thus, for Bataille, "the obscene" simultaneously revives what is most painful and scores a victory over that pain. And of necessity, he must deal with the extremity of the erotic experience. Human beings, he says in the essay part of *Madame Edwarda,* live only through "excess." And pleasure depends on "perspective," or giving oneself to a state of "open being," open to death as well as to joy. Most people, Bataille notes, try to outwit their own feelings; they want to be receptive to pleasure but keep "horror" at a distance. That's foolish, he argues, since horror reinforces "attraction" and excites desire.

What the extremity of the erotic experience means for Bataille is its subterranean connection with death. It's not that Bataille litters his narratives with corpses. (For instance, only one person dies in the terrifying *Histoire de l'Oeil;* and the book ends with the three central characters, having debauched their way through France and Spain, acquiring a yacht at Gibraltar to pursue their infamies elsewhere.) What Bataille does is more effective. He invests each action with a weight, a disturbing gravity, that feels authentically "mortal."

Yet despite the obvious differences of scale and finesse of execution, there are some resemblances between the conceptions of Sade and Bataille. For instance, Sade, like Bataille, was not so much a sensualist as someone with an intellectual project: to explore the scope of transgression. And he shares with Bataille the same ultimate identification of sex and death. But Sade could never have written what Bataille did: "The truth of eroticism is tragic." People often die in Sade's books. But these deaths never seem real. They're no more convincing than those mutilations inflicted during the evening's orgies from which the victims recover completely the next morning following the use of a wondrous salve. One is continually caught up short by Sade's bad faith about death. (Of course, many pornographic books which are much less interesting and accomplished than those of Sade share this bad faith.)

Indeed, one might speculate that the fatiguing repetitiveness of Sade's books is the consequence of his imaginative failure to confront the inevitable goal or haven of a truly systematic venture of the pornographic imagination. Death is the only end to the odyssey of the pornographic imagination when it becomes systematic; that is, when it comes to be focused on the pleasures of transgression rather than mere pleasure itself. Since he could not or would not arrive at his ending, Sade stalled. He multiplied and thickened his narrative; tediously reduplicated orgiastic permutations and combinations. And he regularly interrupted a bout of rape or buggery to deliver to his victims his latest reworkings of lengthy sermons on what real "Enlightenment" means— the nasty truth about God, society, nature, the individual, virtue. Bataille manages to eschew anything resembling the counter-idealisms which are Sade's blasphemies (and thereby perpetuate the banished idealism lying behind those fantasies); his blasphemies are autonomous.

Sade's books, the Wagnerian music-dramas of pornographic literature, are neither subtle nor compact. Bataille achieves his effects with far more economical means: a chamber ensemble of noninterchangeable personages instead of Sade's operatic multiplication of sexual virtuosi and professional victims. Extreme compression is the artistic means which Bataille chooses to render his radical negatives. And it works. This is why Bataille's lean work and gnomic thought go farther than Sade's. Even in pornography, less can be more.

Bataille also has offered distinctly original and effective solutions to one of the perennial formal problems of pornographic narration: the ending. The most common procedure has been an end which lay no claim to any internal necessity. Hence, Adorno remarked that pornography has neither beginning, middle, nor end. But it does. That the end is abrupt and, by conventional novel standards, unmotivated, is

160   SUSAN SONTAG

science-fiction novel, of an alien planet may be no less abrupt or unmotivated.) Abruptness, an endemic facticity of
encounters and chronically renewing encounters, is not some
unfortunate defect of the pornographic narration which one
might wish removed in order for the books to qualify as literature. These features are constitutive of the very imagination or vision of the world which goes into pornography.
They supply, in many cases, exactly the ending that's
needed.

But this doesn't preclude other types of endings. One not-
able feature of *Histoire de l'Oeil* and, to a lesser extent, *The
Image,* considered as works of art, is their attempt to find
more systematic or rigorous kinds of ending. And to do this,
still within the terms of the pornographic imagination; not
seduced by the solutions of a more realistic or less abstract
fiction.

What seems to be entailed is the construction of a narrative which is, from the beginning, more rigorously controlled; less spontaneous and lavishly descriptive.

In *The Image* the narrative is controlled by a single metaphor, "the image" (though the reader doesn't understand the
full meaning of the title until he has reached the end of the
novel). At first, the metaphor appears to have a clear single
application. "Image" seems to be used in the sense of "flat"
object or "two-dimensional surface" or "passive reflection"
—all referring to the girl Anne whom Claire instructs the
narrator to use freely for his own sexual purposes, making
the girl into "a perfect slave." But exactly in the middle of
the book ("Section V" in a short book of ten sections), an
enigmatic scene is interposed which introduces another sense
of "image." Claire, alone with the narrator, wants to show
him a set of strangely unintelligible photographs of Anne in
obscene situations; and these are described in such a way as
to insinuate a mystery in what has been a brutally straightforward, if seemingly unmotivated, situation. From this
cæsura forward to the end of the book, the reader will have

to carry simultaneously the awareness of the fictionally actual "obscene" situation being described and of some kind of oblique mirroring or reduplication of that situation. That burden (the two perspectives) will then be relieved in the final pages of the book, when, as the title of the last section has it, "Everything Resolves Itself." Anne is discovered to be not the erotic plaything of Claire donated gratuitously to the narrator, but Claire's "image" or "projection," sent out ahead to teach the narrator how to love *her*.

The structure of *Histoire de l'Oeil* is no less rigorous, and more ambitious in scope. It's interesting that both novels are in the first person; in both, the narrator is male, and one of a trio whose sexual interconnections constitute the story of the book. But the principles by which the two narratives are organized don't resemble each other at all. "Jean de Berg" describes how something came to be known that was not known by the narrator; all the pieces of action are clues, bits of evidence; and the ending is a surprise. Bataille is describing an action which is really intrapsychic: three people sharing (without conflict) a single fantasy, the acting out of a collective perverse will. The emphasis in *The Image* is on behavior, which is opaque, unintelligible. The emphasis in *Histoire de l'Oeil* is on fantasy first, and then on its correlation with some spontaneously "invented" act. The development of the book follows the phases of acting out. Bataille is charting the stages of the gratification of an erotic obsession, which haunts a number of commonplace objects or things. The principle of organization is thus a spatial one: a series of objects, arranged in a definite sequence, are tracked down, used or used up in some convulsive erotic act. The obscene playing with or defiling of these objects, and of people in their vicinity, is the action of the novella. When the last object (the eye) is used up in a transgression more daring than any preceding, the narrative ends. There can be no revelation or surprises in the story, no new "knowledge," only further intensifications of what is already known. These seemingly unrelated elements really are related; in fact, all versions of the same thing. The egg in the first chapter is simply the first version of the eyeball plucked from the Spaniard in the last.

Each specific erotic fantasy is also a generic fantasy, of performing what is "forbidden," which generates a surplus atmosphere of excruciating restless sexual intensity. At times the reader seems to be witness to a heartless debauched fulfillment; at other times, simply in attendance at the remorseless progress of the negative. Bataille's works, better than any others I know of, indicate the esthetic possibilities of pornography as an art form. *Histoire de l'Oeil* is, in my opinion, the most perfect artistically of all the pornographic prose fictions I've read; *Madame Edwarda,* the most original and powerful intellectually.

To speak of the esthetic possibilities of pornography as an art form and as a form of thinking may seem insensitive or grandiose when one thinks of the acute misery of those afflicted in real life with a full-time specialized sexual obsession. Still, I would argue that pornography yields more than the truths of individual nightmare. Convulsive and repetitious as this form of the imagination may be, it does generate a vision of the world that can claim the interest (speculative, esthetic) of those who are not erotomanes. Indeed, this claim resides in precisely what are customarily dismissed as the *limits* of pornographic thinking.

V

The prominent characteristic of all products of the pornographic imagination is their energy and their absolutism.

The books generally called pornographic are books whose primary, exclusive, and overriding preoccupation is with the depiction of sexual "intentions" and "activities." One could also say sexual "feelings," except that the word seems redundant. For most of the personages deployed by the pornographic imagination, their "feelings" at any given moment are either identical with their "behavior" or else a preparatory phase, that of "intention," just about to break into "behavior" unless physically thwarted. There is a small crude vocabulary of feeling, all relating to the prospects of action. One feels that one would like to act (lust). One feels that one would not like to act (shame, fear). There are no gratuitous or nonfunctioning feelings; no musings, whether speculative or imagistic, which are irrelevant to the business at hand. Thus, the pornographic imagination inhabits a universe that is, however repetitive the incidents which occur within it, incomparably economical. The strictest possible criterion of relevance applies: everything must somehow bear upon the erotic situation.

The universe proposed by the pornographic imagination is a total universe. It has the power to ingest and metamorphose and translate all concerns that are fed into it, reducing everything into the one negotiable currency of the erotic imperative. All action is conceived of as a set of sexual *exchanges*. Thus, the reason why pornography refuses to make fixed distinctions between the sexes or allow any kind of sexual preference or sexual taboo to endure can be explained "structurally." The bisexuality, the disregard for the incest taboo, and other similar features common to pornographic narratives function to multiply the possibilities of exchange. Ideally, it should be possible for everyone to have a sexual connection with everyone else.

Of course the pornographic imagination is hardly the only form of the imagination that proposes a total universe. Another example is the type of imagination that has generated modern symbolic logic. In the total universe proposed by the logician's imagination, all statements can be broken down or chewed up to make it possible to rerender them in the form of the logical language; those parts of ordinary language that don't fit are simply lopped off. Certain of the well known states of the religious imagination, to take another example, operate in the same cannibalistic way, engorging all materials made available to them for retranslation into phenomena saturated with the religious polarities (sacred and profane, etc.).

The latter example, for obvious reasons, touches closely to the present subject. Religious metaphors abound in a good deal of modern erotic literature (in Genet, among others) and in some works of pornographic literature, too. *Story of O,* particularly, is filled with religious metaphors for the ordeal that O undergoes. O "wanted to believe." Her drastic condition of total personal servitude to those who use her sexually is repeatedly described as a mode of salvation. With anguish and anxiety, she surrenders herself; and "henceforth there were no more hiatuses, no dead time, no remission." While she has, to be sure, entirely lost her freedom, O has gained the right to participate in what is described as virtually a sacramental rite.

> *The word "open" and the expression "opening her legs" were, on her lover's lips, charged with such uneasiness and power that she could never hear them without experiencing a kind of internal prostration, a sacred submission, as though a god, and not he, had spoken to her.*

Though she fears the whip and other cruel mistreatments before they are inflicted on her, "yet when it was over she was happy to have gone through it, happier still if it had been especially cruel and prolonged." The whipping, branding, and mutilating are described (from the point of view of *her* consciousness) as ritual ordeals which test the faith of someone being initiated into an ascetic spiritual discipline. The "perfect submissiveness" that her original lover, and then Sir Stephen, demand of her seems to echo the extinction of the self explicitly required of a Jesuit novice or Zen pupil. O is "that absent-minded person who has yielded up her will in order to be totally remade," to be made fit to serve a will far more powerful and authoritative than her own.

As might be expected, the straightforwardness of the religious metaphors in *Story of O* has evoked some correspond-

ingly straight readings of the book. The novelist Mandiargues, whose preface precedes Paulhan's in the American
translation just published, doesn't hesitate to describe *Story
of O* as "a mystic work," and therefore "not, strictly speaking, an erotic book." What *Story of O* depicts "is a complete
spiritual transformation, what others would call an *ascesis*."
But the matter is not so simple. He's right to dismiss an
analysis of O's state of mind in psychiatric terms that would
reduce the book's subject to, say, "masochism." As Paulhan
says, "the heroine's ardor" is totally inexplicable in terms of
the conventional psychiatric vocabulary. The fact that the
novel employs some of the conventional motifs and trappings of the theater of sadomasochism has itself to be explained. But then, Mandiargues has fallen into an error
which is no less reductive and only slightly less vulgar.
Surely, the only alternative to the psychiatric reductions is
not the religious vocabulary. But that only these two foreshortened alternatives exist can, perhaps, be explained as yet
one more echo of the bone-deep denigration of the range
and seriousness of sexual experience that still rules this culture, for all its much-advertised new permissiveness.

My own view is that "Pauline Réage" wrote an erotic
book. The notion implicit in *Story of O* that eros is a sacra-
ment is not the "truth" behind the literal (erotic) sense of
the book—the lascivious rites of enslavement and degradation performed upon O—but, exactly, a metaphor for it.
Why say something stronger, when the statement can't really
mean anything stronger? But despite the virtual incompre-
hensibility to most educated people today of the substantive
experience behind religious vocabulary, there is a continuing piety toward the grandeur of emotions that went into
that vocabulary. The religious imagination survives for most
people as not just the primary, but virtually the only credi-
ble instance of an imagination working in a total way.

No wonder, then, that the new or radically revamped
forms of the total imagination which have arisen in the past
century—notably, those of the artist, the erotomane, and

the madman—have chronically tended to borrow from the prestige of the religious vocabulary. And total experiences, of which there are many kinds, tend again and again to be apprehended only as revivals or translations of the religious imagination. To try to make a fresh way of talking at the most serious, ardent, and enthusiastic level, heading off the religious encapsulation, is one of the primary intellectual tasks of future thought. As matters stand, with everything from *Story of O* to Mao reabsorbed into the incorrigible survival of the religious impulse, all thinking and feeling gets devalued. (Hegel made perhaps the grandest attempt to create a postreligious vocabulary, out of philosophy, that would command the treasures of passion and credibility and emotive appropriateness that were gathered into the religious vocabulary. But his most interesting followers steadily undermined the abstract meta-religious language in which he had bequeathed his thought, and concentrated instead on the specific social and practical applications of his revolutionary form of process-thinking, historicism. Hegel's failure lies like a gigantic disturbing hulk across the intellectual landscape. And no one has been big enough, pompous enough, or energetic enough since Hegel to attempt the task again.)

And so we remain, careening among our overvaried choices of kinds of total imagination, of species of total seriousness. Perhaps the deepest spiritual resonance of the career of pornography in its "modern" Western phase under consideration here (pornography in the Orient or the Moslem world being a very different set of phenomena) is this vast frustration of human passion and seriousness since the old religious imagination, and its secure monopoly on the total imagination, began in the late eighteenth century to crumble. The ludicrousness and lack of skill of most pornographic writing, films, etc., is well known to everyone who has been exposed to them. What is less often remarked about the typical products of the pornographic imagination is their pathos. Most pornography—the books discussed here cannot be excepted—points to something more general than even sexual damage. I mean the traumatic failure of modern capitalist society to provide authentic outlets for the perennial human flair for high-temperature visionary obsessions, to satisfy the appetite for exalted self-transcending modes of concentration and seriousness. The need of human beings to transcend "the personal" is no less profound than the need to be a person, an individual. But this society serves that need poorly. It provides mainly demonic vocabularies in which to situate that need and from which to initiate action and construct rites of behavior. One is offered a choice among vocabularies of thought and action which are not merely self-transcending but self-destructive.

VI

But the pornographic imagination is not just to be understood as a form of psychic absolutism—some of whose products we might be able to regard (in the role of connoisseurs, rather than clients) with more sympathy or intellectual curiosity or esthetic sophistication.

Several times before in this essay I have alluded to the possibility that the pornographic imagination says something, albeit in a degraded and often unrecognizable form, worth listening to. I've suggested that this spectacularly cramped form of the human imagination has, nevertheless, its peculiar access to some truth. And this truth—about sensibility, about sex, about individual personality, about despair, about limits—can be shared when it projects itself into art. (Everyone, at least in dreams, has inhabited the world of the pornographic imagination for some hours or days or even longer periods of his life; but it's the full-time residents who make the fetishes, the trophies, the art.) That something one might call the poetry of transgression is also knowledge. He who transgresses not only breaks a rule. He goes somewhere that the others are not, and he knows something the others don't know.

Pornography, considered as an artistic or art-producing

form of the human imagination, is an expression of what William James called "morbid-mindedness." But James was surely right when he gave as part of the definition of morbid-mindedness that it ranged over "a wider scale of experience" than healthy-mindedness.

What can be said, though, to the many sensible and sensitive people who find depressing the fact that a whole library of pornographic reading material has been made, within the last few years, so easily available in paperback form to the very young? Probably one thing: that their apprehension is justified, but may not be in scale. I am not addressing the usual complainers, those who feel that since sex, after all, *is* dirty, so are books reveling in sex (dirty in a way that a genocide screened nightly on TV, apparently, is not). There still remains a sizeable minority of people who object to or are repelled by pornography not because they think it's dirty, but because they know how pornography can be a crutch for the psychologically deformed and a brutalization of the morally innocent. I dislike pornography for those reasons, too, and feel uncomfortable about the consequences of its increasing availability. But isn't the worry somewhat misplaced? What's really at stake? A concern about the uses of knowledge itself. There's a sense in which *all* knowledge is dangerous, the reason being that not everyone is in the same condition as knowers or potential knowers. Perhaps most people don't need "a wider scale of experience." It may be that, without subtle and extensive psychic preparation, any widening of experience and consciousness is destructive for most people. Then we must ask what justifies the reckless unlimited confidence we have in the present mass availability of other kinds of knowledge, in our optimistic acquiescence in the transformation of and extension of human capacities by machines. Pornography is only one item among the many dangerous commodities being circulated in this society; unattractive as it may be, it's probably one of the less lethal, the less costly to the community in terms of human suffering. Except perhaps in a small circle of writer-intellectuals in France, pornography is an inglorious and mostly despised department of the imagination. Its mean status is the very antithesis of the considerable spiritual prestige enjoyed by many items which are far more noxious.

In the last analysis, the place we assign to pornography depends on the goals we set for our own consciousness, our own experience. But the goal A subscribes to for his consciousness may *not* be one he's pleased to see B adopt, because he judges that B isn't qualified or experienced or subtle enough. And B may be dismayed and even indignant at A's adopting goals that he himself professes; when A holds them, they become presumptuous or shallow. Surely this chronic mutual suspicion of our neighbor's capacities—suggesting, in effect, a hierarchy of competence with respect to human consciousness—won't ever be settled to every one's satisfaction. When the quality of people's consciousness varies so greatly, how could it ever be?

In an essay on the subject some years ago, Paul Goodman wrote: "The question is not *whether* pornography, but the quality of the pornography." That's exactly right. One could extend the thought a good deal further. The question is not *whether* consciousness or *whether* knowledge, but the quality of the consciousness and of the knowledge. And that invites consideration of the quality or fineness of the human subject—the most problematic standard of all. It doesn't seem inaccurate to say most people in this society who aren't actively mad are, at best, reformed or potential lunatics. But is anyone supposed to act on this knowledge, even genuinely live with it? If so many are teetering on the verge of murder, dehumanization, sexual deformity and despair, and we were to act on that thought, then censorship much more radical than the indignant critics of pornography ever envisage seems in order. For if that's the case, not only pornography but all forms of serious art and knowledge—in other words, all forms of truth—are suspect and dangerous.

Felix Pollak

Pornography: A Trip Around the Halfworld

I

PORNOGRAPHY AND ITS SIAMESE TWIN, CENSORSHIP, ARE PROB-lems and as such, by definition, beyond solutions; whatever can be resolved and put into a polyethylene bag is no prob-lem. I could begin by saying that I am, in principle, against censorship of any kind (but of course!) and you need not be afraid that I'll continue the sentence by saying, "but you have to draw the line *somewhere.*" It's worse than that: I have, right in the face of my principle, to make a case also *for* censorship. The reconciliation lies in the fact that I am *for* pornography. Let me explain.

On the one hand, the text of the Federal Obscenity Statute, 18 U.S.C.§1461, breaks me up. There are few funnier passages in English literature than this judicial swear & sputter:

> *Every obscene, lewd, lascivious, indecent, filthy or vile article, matter, thing, device, or substance; and . . . every written or printed card, letter, circular, book, pamphlet, advertisement, or notice of any kind, giving information, directly or indirectly, where, or how, from whom, or by what means of, such mentioned matters . . . may be obtained . . . is declared to be non-mailable matter and shall not be conveyed in the mails, or delivered from any post office or by any letter carrier, etc.*

I like the sound of this, the rhythm, the alliterations, the redundancies engendered by the legalistic quest for all-inclusiveness and water-tightupness. The joke is that it means nothing because it defines nothing; sinister sounds and invectives are no substitutes for tangible criteria. And it means nothing also because a person can be found guilty and jailed as a purveyor of pornography without purveying anything pornographic. This may sound paradoxical but is literally true: I am of course referring to the Supreme Court decision of October 1965 in the case of Ralph Ginzburg.

Neither the magazine *Eros* which Ginzburg edited, nor his biweekly newsletter *Liaison,* nor "Rey Anthony's" book *The Housewife's Handbook on Selective Promiscuity* of which he was the publisher was judged pornographic; the reason given for the five-year jail term the Court imposed on the defendant was that he advertised these publications in a suggestive manner; that in his publicity he was, in the Court's phrase, "pandering to the widespread weakness for titillation by pornography."

I don't want to go into the matter—that has sufficiently been done. I don't want to carry a torch for Mr. Ginzburg, who surely is no courageous literary avant-gardist but merely a fast-buck artist. I don't want to be led astray by attaching the question, "And what's wrong with that?" to the Supreme

Court's definition of Ginzburg's "offense." I don't even want
to dwell on Justice Douglas's dry remark in his dissenting
opinion that the criterion of prurient advertising of nonpru-
rient matter could make *The Song of Solomon* a pornographic product. (What I *might* say, in passing, is—and
none of the dissenting judges, surprisingly, has pointed this
out—that a truly pornographic book could also be de-por-
nographed according to that criterion, by a publisher's simple device of ceasing to advertise it, or by changing the tone
of the advertising from low to high.) My main point here,
however, is this: if the substance of a piece of writing is to be
judged pornographic, the Federal Obscenity Statute, even
with the vague and relative criterion of "community standards" thrown in, is useless in determining it; and if the
advertising—nowhere, heretofore, set down as a criterion
—is to be made the guide, then 90 per cent of the advertisers in this country ought to be in jail. (Which, for other reasons, might not be a bad idea.)

Who has said "on the one hand" must say "on the other
hand." So here we go: On the other hand, censorship does
have a case. The typical liberal, inveighing against censorship, is likely to cite the old saw, "No girl has ever been seduced by a book." This, I believe, is an erroneous statement;
I sincerely hope it is. For the saying doesn't do the cause of
literature any good, or the intellectual cause in general. If
one denies the power of the word to do evil, one denies the
power of the word to do good. In effect, one denies the
power of the word. I prefer the healthy fear and awe of the
written and spoken word, evidenced by censorious zealots, to
the wishy-washy neutralism of the liberalist anticensors. For
better or worse, in sickness and in health, words *have* influenced the actions of men, after all—from the Ten Com-
mandments to *Mein Kampf,* from *Il Principe* to *Das Kapital,* from the *Contrat Social* to the *Traumlehre,* from Lu-
ther's Fourteen Theses to the Bill of Rights. When *Die Lei-
den des jungen Werthers* appeared, a wave of suicides is said
to have swept the land, and when Nora closed the door to
the Doll's House, the emancipation of women had begun in

earnest. So, while censorship is nefarious and based on the folly that thoughts, manifesting themselves in words, can be suppressed instead of merely modified or supplanted by more appealing thoughts, the would-be censors at least take thoughts and words seriously; and that is more than can be said of many of the liberalists who seem not even aware of their dilemma.

But the typical liberalist's dilemma goes still deeper. Anxious to protect a work accused of pornography, he normally sets out to prove that it isn't pornographic at all. This has been the traditional pattern in court case after court case, and it is to be found in literary criticism as well. The attorneys for the defense and their expert witnesses may be compelled to take that stance in order to prevail in a court of law. But it is a hypocritical subterfuge nevertheless.[1] Instead of frankly admitting that a book may be pornographic and in spite of it, or even because of it, a good book, they endeavor to argue pornography away altogether. Listening to them, you get the impression that there is no such thing as pornography. And they may yet bring about that state of affairs, and a sad state of affairs it will be. Where everything is permitted and nothing forbidden, there is no more sin. But as already Adam and Eve knew, the forbidden fruit tasted so sweet precisely because it was forbidden. If that apple had been like any other apple on any other tree, they would have never known the difference, and we'd all still be in paradise, bored to death. (Or perhaps, since they wouldn't have started begetting then, we wouldn't even be here.)

A point of view more to my taste and much more honest and realistic has been succinctly expressed some years ago in the Canadian little magazine *Delta*. The brief piece by Alden A. Nowlan is titled "A Defense of Obscenity" and reads in part:

> Nobody has ever defined obscenity satisfactorily. But one of the most common definitions is that obscenity is whatever incites lust. Judges, customs officers, cabinet ministers, Sun-

[1] See notes at the end of this essay, p. 195.

*day School teachers and other sachems of the Anglo-Saxon
kith generally agree that if a book arouses the libidinous
instinct it is obscene. The assumption seems to be acceptable to publishers too. They usually defend their questionable books on the grounds that the sections which alarm the
censors are literary or clinical descriptions which would not
arouse a normal, adult reader. Such a definition of obscenity could exist only in a society which hates and fears sex.
The fear and hate are so ferocious, in fact, that not even
the most liberal opponents of censorship argue that it may
be good for the reader to have his libidinous instincts excited occasionally. And even the frankest authors don't announce that it is their ambition to further literature and
serve society by writing a book so obscene that it will be an
infallible aphrodisiac.*

   *Once we reject the perverse and curious Anglo-Saxon
conception of sex which is literally that it is a necessary
evil, it's obvious that a certain amount of a certain kind of
obscenity in certain types of books is a good thing.*

This view of pornography and sex in general is opposed to
two other points of view, both out to kill with kindness: the
view of the whitewashers who would also prove that there
really is no such thing as prostitution, "that most useful of
human institutions," as Gore Vidal says, but that whores actually are either maligned philanthropists or slightly eccentric artistic types to whom one has to grant, like to Hollywood actresses, a certain leeway in matters of morality; and
the view of the detached scientist who places copulating couples in an armor of wiring to record their responses on
graphs and charts, who measures the rhythms of ejaculation
and catches the sperm in test tubes to find out whether its
fertilizing capacity is affected by the intensity of the orgasm.

   This is the end of the sex act as an act of enjoyment, just
as the assigned reading of *Ulysses* or of *Lolita* in English 201
is the end of aphrodisiac reading, as far as these two books
are concerned. To read *Tropic of Cancer* after smuggling it
in from Paris, and to read it after buying a paperback copy
in the supermarket are two entirely different things. I, for

one, deplore its open availability: not from a moralistic, but from an anti-moralistic point of view. Once, when one had to buy it under the counter and read it undercover, disguised by an innocuous dustjacket, it was a sin and a lustful experience; now it has lost its punch, it has become a part of our mass civilization.

Sex, in other words, is neither sex hygiene, nor sociology, nor psychology, nor psychiatry, nor science, nor medicine, nor literature; at least not Literature with a capital L. In pornography, the sexual word is a sexual act. In Litchacha it is exegesis, commentary, analysis, criticism; immured, emasculated, altered, neutered; not life, but life-like. All this sounds obvious, but isn't. Our attitudes toward sex and pornography prove it. Henry Miller, who should know, has stated the case in *Quiet Days in Clichy:* "The sexual life flourishes better in a dim, murky light; it is at home in the chiaroscuro and not in the glare of the neon light."

This is, in the face of all my rebelliousness against repression, my case in favor of censorship. As long as freedom can fight against limits, there is freedom; unlimited freedom negates itself, is merely an aimless tumbling in outer space. Pornography, in a climate of utter permissiveness, is *ipso facto* obliterated. And we can see the consequences all around us. I am convinced that the guilt-edged Victorians and Puritans had much more fun than we have in our sensational, hypersensational, hyper-duper-super sensational, guiltless, jaded sexual liberty that is forever vainly trying to outdo itself, with and without drugs. Basically, it is a quest for guilt, for limitations, for prohibitions that will permit trespasses and transgressions. ("Then I remembered my desire for infamy, or rather that it was infamous I had at all costs to be," says the protagonist in Georges Bataille's *Madame Edwarda*.) The increasing accent in pornographic and semipornographic literature on the sadomasochistic syndrome is quite possibly a facet of our quest for proscriptions and punishment.

The Victorians, I started to say, were living in an atmosphere of constant sinful and lustful tension, with evil and seduction lurking in every dark corner and right above a woman's ankle, should an inch of it show as she entered a carriage; and what delicious shivers up and down their spines they must have felt in spotting the bottom of a girl bending over to pick a flower! Now, with miniskirts all over town and bikinis abounding on every beach and mammalian tits popping out of subway posters and movie screens and hanging into the cocktails served by topless waitresses, the best one can get out of all this is a soft-on, as Paul Krassner calls it. I vividly remember the boredom I felt in a joint on Place Pigalle, where sexual stimulation surely was intended, watching an endless array of bare buttocks and breasts passing by me on a stage a few feet away, monotonous and as cold as the frozen smiles on the uniform lips of the paraders. It resembled an army inspection or an anatomy class, and I kept thinking what a pleasant shock just one scantily dressed girl would have provided. It is the veiled and forbidden that entices. "Raw" nudity is actually not raw at all but dull, and nudist colonies must be the most sexless places on earth. As Bernard Shaw observed, if you really want to abolish sex, go stark naked. Where there is no resistance, there is no allure.

II

To go into some detail, we might apply the above observations to sexual words, to pornographic words, to the euphemistically called fourletter words. As miniskirts proliferate in city streets, so fourletter words proliferate in current literature, to the point of becoming commonplace, accepted, not warranting a second look. Which in my opinion is a pity. They used to be called, and were, dirty words; now their apologists and casual practitioners can't even refer to them without putting "dirty" in quotes, as if to say, there ain't no such thing. And when they get through with them, there isn't. And again they are aided and abetted by rationalistic and detached philologists and etymologists, by "mature" and "enlightened" and shockproof sophisticates, and by—hold everything!—clergymen.

In *Sex as a Gift—a Guide to Young People* (see what I mean?), the Reverend Ian Fraser, connected with the Scottish Churches House, writes:

> Fuck *was simply a descriptive word, commonly in use among the common people: a word which represented a human act in a quite unloaded way. Prejudice against it was largely class prejudice. Timidity in its use derived largely from a traditional timidity. The word could be restored if we had the courage to restore it, and could do useful service in the future as it had in the past.*

Well, here is where I came in. After this, "fuck" might do useful service in a quite unloaded way (how true!), but I doubt that it can ever be restored to what it used to be, say, in the days of Mark Twain. (Who, in his class prejudice and traditional timidity, to my knowledge never used it in print.)

There simply is such a thing as word magic and the power of the taboo. The German phrase, *den Teufel nicht an die Wand malen,* let's not draw a picture of the devil on the wall, testifies to the belief that the symbol can conjure up the real thing. The power of unholy as well as of holy names wanes of course if they're spoken in vain; overuse brings ever diminishing returns, and after the first few pages of many current novels, plays, and hippie poetry, there is about as much sexuality left in the limited vocabulary of obscenity the English language can boast as there is in the act of undressing for an operation.

Looking through recent little magazines and their latest mutation, the "underground" tabloid, one is struck with another strange thing about the Anglo-American usage of those Anglo-Saxon words. It is the fact that they're used for anything, from cussing to meaningless adjectival description, rather than for their basic meaning. This had startled me already when I, the foreign-born, first encountered them in the U.S. Army, and the observation can be made on any street and in any bar. There is an army joke illustrating the point: One soldier tells a buddy how he had left the fucking barracks and taken a fucking bus to the fucking town and gone into a fucking saloon and had a few fucking beers and then spotted that there fucking broad and bought her a fucking drink and finally took her to a fucking hotel and tore off her fucking dress and threw her on the fucking bed. "And then?" asks his buddy, his tongue hanging out. "Well," says the soldier, "then, natch, we had sexual intercourse." There is no exaggeration in this. My comrades-in-arms asked routinely to please pass the fucking butter and joyfully reported that someone's fucking sister was still a fucking virgin, and that someone else's fucking wife had just had another fucking baby. They advised one another, either politely or angrily, to go fuck themselves, without any expectation that their advice would or could be heeded; they commiserated with someone who had been fucked out of a deal and agreed that things in general were all fucked up. Etc. There seems no end to the usages of that word, all far removed from its original sense. The phrase "snafu" has become part of the vocabulary in the "best" society and many users seem quite unaware of what it stands for. And even if the primary meaning crops up, it is more often than not equated with other meanings or no meanings. I just recently read in a story in one of the above-mentioned not so underground newspapers—I forget whether it was the *Berkeley Barb* or the *East Village Other* or *Oracle* or the *Fifth Estate* or such—a dialogue in the course of which one boy confided to another that he would like to get fucked. "Not in this fucking town, you can't," was the reply. (And I don't think this was meant satirically.)

It seems to me here is a new kind of Puritanism at work. The change of the sexual connotation into asexual ones is a mechanism of evasion that manifests itself also in the softening of the spelling into "fug"—a word that has evidently been made quite socially acceptable by the popularity of The Fugs, the band of folksingers founded by Ed Sanders, the editor of *Fuck You: A Magazine of the Arts*. There are Fug records and Fug shirts, and when The Fugs come to a college town, the hall where they appear is overflowing, minks mingling with housewifely dresses and jeans and everybody, from co-ed to matron, saying "fug, fug, fug." It would be funny if it weren't sad. The dirty words—and "fuck" is not alone in this—are all washed up, and we shall all rise now for a minute of silent mourning.

I am actually serious about this. I believe the taboo word springs from a deep need of the human psyche, and if the symbols responding to that need become ineffective, a new set of taboo expressions will evolve. Sanders, who has a kind of ribald wit, has been coining some candidates in his various bizarre publications, mostly onomatopoeic and occasionally onomatopoetic terms like "gobble-slurp," "zap," "petzel-hassles," "glit," etc., but the fact of the matter is, there is no such thing as an esperanto of obscenity, an artificially created forbidden language. Whimsical and scurrilous coinages are good for a laugh, but they are not what Eugene Jolas called "night words"—though that term connoted more than just sexual taboo symbols. Sea water cannot be produced by adding salt to lake water; salty and earthy speech is, like all language, an organic growth. The dictionaries of slang are perhaps nearer to the evolvement of language than Webster's or the Oxford English, but even they are like nets dredging the ocean of words and coming up with a relatively small haul of slithering, still live fishes, letting most of the small but vital fry of big-fishes-to-be slip through the mesh.[2]

III

What I am arguing, then, is that the wholesale bestowal of permissiveness is more deadly to pornography as a genre than the barbs of ostracism and the shackles of censorship. The sophisticates are killing pruriency with sanctimoniousness, and the only people who still succeed in giving the public a surreptitious thrill are at the moment the Los Angeles cops who doggedly arrest each night the performers of

[2] See notes at the end of this essay, p. 196.

McClure's *The Beard,* a play abounding in fourletter words
as well as fourletter acts, all pronounced and enacted on a
stage. The audience, expecting kicks and no doubt getting
them from a sensational, scandal-laden atmosphere in which
policemen provide the delicious element of anything-can-
happen, is crowding every performance and thus enables the
actors to pay, regularly and with equal doggedness after each
night's arrest, the bail money the police extorts from them,
so they may play another night. Like virtually everything in
America, this set-up has developed into big business and
thereby acquired a legitimacy of its own—an illegitimate
legitimacy, so to speak. And so, an enjoyable and lucrative
time is had by all, and will be, until everybody directly or
indirectly connected with the spectacle will have his day in
court. Should the verdict be an acquittal and the performance be set free, minus cops and minus the lure of infamy,
the play will most likely die of its freedom soon thereafter.

When I grew up in Vienna, the members of the middle
class were apt to view sex as a kind of venereal disease of
which one speaks only in whispers. Their attitude was
abhorrent. But still more abhorrent was the self-righteous-
ness of the social reformers who rose to the defense of sexual
freedom. Suffragette types, as zealous as they were shapeless,
rallied to preach the gospel of free-thinking; spouseless, they
espoused the ideal of free love and free divorce; spinsters
with pincenez embraced the cause of the untrammeled libido, took the *id* onto their flat bosoms, declared war on the
superego, and in general lisped and shrieked about Eros the
way a blind man talks about colors. The only escape from either fright was to the ladies of uneasy virtue and to the
books of easy vice. And vice has its virtues.

In an article in *The New Republic,* titled "An Apology
for Pornography," Peter Michelson says, "Pornography . . .
is the imaginative record of man's sexual will." I agree, but I
would add, not merely in apology for, but in praise of, pornography, that it represents the triumph of mind over matter, that it distinguishes man from animal. Only man can experience sexual excitement, with all its physical concomi-

tants, including orgasm, by mental stimulation alone. Imagination is a uniquely human attribute, and erotic imagination is surely the most basic and potent of all phantasies.
The possibility of sexual arousal by the printed or spoken
word alone is to me a psychosomatic marvel, reversing, as it
does, the soma-psychological reaction of beast and primitive
man where any semblance of mental enjoyment is dependent
on physical excitation. This complete cause and effect rever-
sal is of course the prerequisite of the sublimation process to
which Freud ascribes the existence of culture. The erotic imagination, however, poses also a threat to society in questioning its values, in pitting man's natural instincts against the
utilitarian standards of tribal morality, in exploding the
myths of man's mono-sexuality and natural monogamy. And
society reacts, permissively or restrictively, according to its
purposes, political structure, and faith in its own tenets.
George P. Elliott,* in an article in *Harper's* titled "Against
Pornography," warns of pornography's nihilistic intent, and
Maurice Girodias, in his preface to *The Olympia Reader,*
and Henry Miller in many utterances before him, rejoice in
that very attack against what they see as our false gods, our
hypocrisies, our neurotic hatred of love and joy. The view of
unlimited sex as the great liberator, the yea-sayer to the life-
force and therefore the nay-sayer to civilization is of course
echoed in many of the current hippie slogans and activities,
the love-ins, the credos of *Make Love, Not War, Copulate
for Coexistence,* etc. The aforementioned Mr. Sanders also
gets into the act, whether in jest or in earnest is hard to tell,
issuing ("zapping & ejaculating") the productions of his
"Fuckpress" under the motto, TOTAL ASSAULT ON
THE CULTURE!

The claim is no doubt greatly exaggerated, as is the simplistic idea that Rome fell because of too much bathing,
drinking, and fornicating. The Scandinavian countries, despite the abundance of pornography all over Copenhagen
and with all the daring and sharply skeptical films being

* See pp. 72–95.

made in Sweden and Norway, seem to be doing all right socially, economically, and politically, and our own society,
too, appears to know, even if only subliminally, that the very
lipservice to which so many of our moral dogmas have been
reduced can be maintained only because pornographic literature and pornographic movies—in the wider sense of the
word that includes the slick, winking, half-veiled, and fully
Hollywood kind of pornography of the *Peyton Place, Carpetbaggers, Candy,* Mickey Spillane, and Hedy Lamarr
variety—permit the maninthestreet and his legalwife the
luxury of living out their sexual wishdreams vicariously,
with the bonus of righteous moral indignation thrown in.

However, the totalitarian and authoritarian countries take
the threat seriously and act predictably different. And the
difference is not the surface one of "freedom of the press" in
a democracy and its lack in a dictatorship. The difference is
the realization of authoritarians—from the Iron Curtain
countries to Castro's Cuba and De Gaulle's France—that
hedonism in all its forms is a humanistic, liberalistic, and individualistic philosophy and as such in opposition to the
"Kadavergehorsam," the social and moral goosestepping,
conformism, and uniformity required by Spartan rule. It is
fascinating to observe the reflection of increasingly stringent
political change in the increasingly stringent moral codes enacted in a country. Soviet Russia began with a demolition of
the bourgeois morality through the most liberal sex views
possible. Free love was a revolutionary slogan and the "glass
of water" theory was actually propagated by the party. It
went like this: if a thirsty man would ask a girl for a glass of
water, wouldn't she, as a good comrade, give it to him? And
if he, thirsty for sex, would ask her for her body, could she,
as a good comrade, deny it to him? It was the right, the
human, the revolutionary, the antibourgeois, the unhypo-
critical thing to do. Today, the USSR is more Puritanical
than America ever was. A recent visitor from East Germany
told me that pornography is as much frowned upon there,
and as ruthlessly suppressed, as heretical political propa-

ganda; they are viewed as merely different manifestations of the same subversiveness. "And if you want to make a lifelong enemy in Leipzig," he added, "and risk your career, all you have to do is to tell an off-color story to the wrong person."

Nothing further needs to be said about the changes that have befallen the traditionally wicked and gay Paree, and Havana, even in Castro's first years still a lecher's paradise. The putas have all become members of the women's auxiliary, one hears—the *army* auxiliary, that is. I must assume that the once so numerous vendors of feelthy pictures have also disappeared from the streets, together with their erstwhile best customers, the American tourists. But the reason is not primarily a need for labor or the official disapproval of prostitution as a capitalistic exploitation (sexploitation) of poor working-class women. The knowledge was too common that many of the whores enjoyed their whoring and the lazy *dolce vita* that went with it; and that they did considerably better financially than the state could begin to do for them. The primary reason for the new puritanisms is the realization that pleasure and discipline don't mix, unless the pleasure, too, is controlled from above, like Hitler's *Kraft durch Freude*. Only then can it be made useful and unthreatening for the government. Moral dissoluteness, it's true, may lead to political dissoluteness, to discontent with austerity, to civil disobedience; the enjoyments of pornography, of masturbation, even of copulating are private acts and as such unwelcome in a collectivistic society and useless to it; unless the copulating can be utilized for breeding, as in the Third Reich. Orwell foresaw all this. There is nothing more fearsome to authority than individualism, anarchism's kissing cousin; nothing more noxious than unorthodox thinking and feeling—thinking and feeling, for short. They have a way of leading to action, the undesirable, uncommandeered, mutinous kind. So, all things considered, the totalitarian state's desire to restrict sexual as well as political liberty is understandable.

The Catholic Church, another authoritarian and totalitar-

ian institution, has from the beginning recognized the
enemy, and for the same reasons. But, more subtle and ingenious than the state, it has discovered a uniquely simple
way of dealing with the problem: it has made the same act
that is an extramarital sin a marital duty. And what can
more effectively take the fun out of anything than making it
a duty—a fucking duty, as it were?

There is, the Church knew, no point in making laws that
will be broken. You can tell people until you're breathless
that sex is for procreation only and not for enjoyment; they
will go on copulating right throughout pregnancy, if physically possible. So you extract as much pleasure as possible
from the act by *extending* the marital duty, illogical and inconsistent as this decree may be. But to secure conformity
and avoid dangerous deviation, you lay down precise rules as
to how and how not, as to the one & only correct position,
the prohibition of "unnatural" mechanical devices, etc. Thus
the practitioners are made to feel that they are performing a
wholesome and required deed with Big Faith Brother standing by and looking down on them, his hands extended in
blessing, and occasionally raised like a conductor's to cau-
tion, *"Piano,* and less staccato, please!"

Children, in other words, will play, and the only method
of controlling their playing is to provide playgrounds for
them and to dampen their exuberance by posting rules and
channeling their games for functional purposes. Functional,
that is, for the supervising agency. The privacy invasion accomplished by those devices is beneficial in itself. The institution of the Confessional is but another mechanism of control, providing the catharsis of pleading guilty and combin-
ing it with the court functions of punishment or acquittal:
all part & parcel of the power complex. Licentiousness in
general, and sexual licentiousness in particular, endangers
the power structure and its strictures, and The Establishment (can you blame it?) fights back, castrating, emasculat-
ing, clipping & nipping in the bud, or trying to.

But here is the irony: pruned saplings grow lush.

IV

They grow in secret, to be sure. If I can trust my informants—and I have every reason to—pornography can be had in any of the Iron-Chastity-Belt countries, most easily in Yugoslavia, though only at prices that bespeak the sellers' risk and the buyers' eagerness. It stands to reason (or emotion). Pressure seeks outlets and, as the Latin proverb recognizes, *naturam expellas furca, tamen usque recurret.* Within pornography—in itself one of the most patent and potent manifestations of expelled nature's eternal return—it is the proven "hard-core" variety that appears to maintain itself most stubbornly and is translated—and pirated—over & over, a kind of survival of the smuttest.

I know nothing about drug use and addiction in totalitarian states but would by analogy venture to guess that it exists also, and perhaps even more intensively, if less extensively, than in the semipermissive West. With us, drugs are means of thrill-seeking, indicative of our expanded consciousness of status symbols, at least in certain sets. In austerer and more regimented societies, escapes into dream worlds of wish fulfillment are more urgent and often the only available metaphors for private rebellion. Governments that require activism of their subjects—an unquestioning, passive kind of activism, that is—must necessarily take a dim view of all drop-out schemes, of all agents of alienation—drugs, pornography, lechery, alcoholism, as well as the most edifying works of literature and art if they're not in the approved category.

L'art pour l'art certainly is anathema to the total state; the functional subservient type of art, on the other hand, is furthered and subsidized. Art has become a new opium for the people—a carefully gauged and controlled vent for letting out the steam of rebellion together with the steam accumulated in the serious business of serving the state. It is a therapeutic precaution, a measure of mental hygiene, like coffee breaks. And allows the regime at the same time to wear its culture-mindedness, backed up by statistics, as a decorative feather in its collectivist cap.

"Degenerate art" (*entartete Kunst,* as it was called in the Third Reich and as it is still called, in various equivalents, by our various authoritarians) is a different matter. Books like *Ulysses* or *Lolita* are, as I found out during a trip abroad last summer, not available in any East German bookstore; not because they're considered dirty, but because they don't contribute anything "useful" to the state.* People can, and should, I was informed, read "more important" books in their spare time; or else "more recreational" ones. Only students and scholars who can prove a professional, preferably critical, interest in them, may borrow these works from the university libraries. It did not occur to me then to inquire about utopias. But I suspect they're equally screened and censored. Utopias are dangerous to the *status quo* (which governments that came into power by revolutions are even more anxious to preserve than their capitalist-bourgeois counterparts). And pornographic books are essentially utopias.

The Marquis de Sade, for example, makes only the feeblest pretense of realism. He was a mathematician of lechery, a compulsive permutationist of sexual experiments, positing a world of orgiastic orgasms, methodically delineated, and forever giving the show away by interspersing intercoursing with discoursing; the philosophical discourses being the *raison d'être* for the intercourses that are to prove and illustrate his theories. And this brings up a question George Steiner raised in an issue of *Encounter* †—a question I had also wondered about: is there a science-fiction pornography?

Here must be a fertile field for the most depraved and bizarre imagination, a real opportunity for the pornographer to come up with something new and utterly outrageous. In a

---

* West Germany, significantly, has its own censorship cases: ludicrous as it sounds, *Fanny Hill* was recently *verboten* at a Munich trial.

† See pp. 96–108.

genre that permits a complete rearrangement of our woebe-
gone world and a remedy of its ills through the simple device of inventing a joybegone new one, you would surely expect to find at least the minimum requirements of sexual
wish-dreaming fulfilled: the enormously intensified and du-
ration-extended orgasm; the nonexistence of impotence and
frigidity and the everlasting, or at least volitional, erection;
the always ready, always lubricated and steaming hot vagina;
the strict separation of the sexual and the procreative functions; and the opportunity of experiencing—hermaphrodit-
ically or otherwise—the male and female sensations simultaneously and cumulatively. Those are really only pedestrian
reforms which do not even envisage copulation-crazy creatures with gigantic, numerous, and varied sex organs indulging in continuous, unheard-of orgies and delights—phantasies with which any self-respecting pornographer ought to
have a ball, or two. And what does Mr. Steiner—one of the
nay-sayers and decriers of pornography—report to have
found? Mutual masturbation between unidentified flying objects! Now that might actually be a first-rate satirical idea,
but as pornography it is from hunger. Already the Byzantine
empress Theodora did better than that, resolving "to satisfy
all amorous orifices of the human body to the full and at the
same time." Mr. Steiner, who quotes her, observes at this
point, drily and justly but without the littlest "alas," that
"there just aren't that many orifices." True, but isn't this
one more reason for the would-be science fiction pornographers (*scificpors*, for short) to create some? What is to stop
them? Except the evident fact that phantasy is no substitute
for imagination. (There is, admittedly, a dampening blanket
here: successful pornography hinges on the reader's ability to
identify with the protagonists and vicariously partake of
their exploits; and it *would* be difficult for a poor human,
limited in organs & orifices, to watch the cavortings of sexual
octopuses without becoming a jealous sourpuss!)

However, don't despair, all is not lost yet. For we have
right on this imperfect planet an institution that has succeeded in establishing a panerotic and often outright porno-

graphic utopia amongst us, embuing every conceivable subject and object with sex and lust: I am referring to the most
respectable pillarofsociety industry of advertising. The difference between its daily practices and those for which
Ralph Ginzburg received a five-year jail term are negligible,
as far as I can see. No differences in kind, minimal ones in
degree. Both types are a rather far cry from the achievements
of Mr. Ed Sanders, who appears to crop up in these contem-
plations, and who issues catalogs of books as well as "literary
relics," "freak-spews," "gobble-vectors," etc., and offers such
items as guaranteed genuine samples of Allen Ginsberg's
pubic hair, paraphernalia used by the East Village greats
and others before, during, and after their sexual hangup, up-
tight and dripdry activities, and who not only gets away with
it but was acquitted in a recent trial. While Mr. Ginzburg
—well, you know. Even more interesting is that our daily &
nightly ad hucksters & hustlers don't even have the need to
be acquitted, because they're never hauled into court in the
first place. My sense of justice would demand that Sanders
remain free, Ginzburg be freed, and they be jailed.

                              V

To substantiate this opinion, let's have a look at the surrounding liminal & subliminal Kingsize Leer. *Time,* the
weekly news magazine (if you'll pardon the expression), does
occasionally come up with something useful and has, some
Time ago, compiled a list that complements my own collection of notes on the subject. To nitwit: the sultry radio
voice, female, whispering hoarsely, "Let it happen, dear . . .
I'll blame (I forget which, choose your brand) perfume." Or
the "Does she . . . or doesn't she?" ads for Miss Clairol. Or
the airline ad on the radio in which a seductress's voice ca-
joles, between casualty figures and race riots, "Skip away to
Florida . . . just the two of you . . . tonight . . . why not?"
Lately, this has been hilariously altered and is alternated, to
catch 'em all, with a male voice's wanting to know, "Going

on a business trip? Mix in a little pleasure—bring your wife along!" A slight pause after this indicates, "Well, if it *should* be your secretary—who are we to tattle on you?" Or the hard female breathing that accompanies a man's Noxema shave and finally foams and bubbles into "Take it off! —take it *all* off!!" *Time* calls such participanting "double entendre" but the singlemindedness of those entendres has long since split them in half, I'd say. I can't, even after three straight martinis, see anything double in the wondering out loud of a hot number asking, "Was it him . . . or his Piping Rock?," or in a flushed hussy's query, "What makes a shy girl get Intimate?" And there is the clothing firm, boasting that it makes suits "for men who make babies." Of course, there is no end to hilarity when it comes to "come"—as when the on-its-last-wheel railroad line tells us "to come with us is the only way to come," while the left-at-home housewife is being seduced by a purring voice promising delights with *Easy-On* (a wallpaper); this is followed (after a brief intermission for the "show") by the commercial for a beer with a "ten-minute head," and is in turn succeeded by two competitive cigaret ads, one assuring you that "It isn't how long you make it but how you make it long," the other prophesying "You make out better at both ends" if only you'll use that magic filter tip; and I have before me a full-page ad from *The New Yorker* "About how and when to drink Harvey's Bristol Cream": it shows on the left a serious elderly gent who, lifting his glass, proclaims, "Straight, is the only way"; but on the right, contradicting him, a winsome wench is cuddling up to a sweatered youth, whispering defiantly, "I like it a couple of different ways, myself." Etc., etc., ad after *ad nauseam.* How much preferable Mr. Sanders's straight-on offers of "dreck & ejaculata," minus all that winking & smirking & innocent fluttering of false eyelashes! The whole talmi-obscene scene, enacted solemnly in the holy name of the fast buck, makes me think of the obsession the witty Austrian writer, Alfred Polgar, ascribed to a painter-friend of his: mountains were exciting to him because they reminded him of breasts and phalluses; valleys were exciting to him because they reminded him of vaginas; but the most exciting of all to him were plains and prairies, because they reminded him of the fusion of convex and concave.

Where the things advertised do in fact serve an erotic purpose, the advertising doesn't necessarily end with the purchase of these articles but continues, in a more intriguing way, through their use. The thing that makes lipsticks, say, or perfumes, alluring to men is not their sight or smell *per se,* but the *intent* behind their use. What they really advertise is the wearer's own erotic interest and potential availability: and *therein* lies their appeal.

Cosmetics, quite obviously, make not even a pretense of trying to enhance nature, to make it more natural looking. Brightly provocative or super-pale lipsticks, drawn to alter a woman's mouth, plainly announce their presence, and so do eyeshades and penciled eyebrows and polished nails. Men know the real shape of a female foot but are entranced, nevertheless, by its appearance in high-heeled pumps, for the high-heeled pumps tell them something that arouses them: the wearer's wish to arouse them. The erotic message of platinum-dyed hair and an insinuating scent is, "I want to be seductive and am seduceable, and while I may enjoy smelling wicked also for myself, it's really for men—for you?— that I put this on." And the made-up-to-by-make-up males respond as expected, listening attentively to the interior and subterranean conversations beneath the trivial or intellectual exchanges, and reciprocating on their own part as well.

But if pornographic advertising is characterized by its incitement of lustful desires, and if the ad can in itself be the pornographic act, then the use of dresses and cosmetics must fall under that definition. Tits are *par excellence* instruments of titillation, especially if displayed in a cunning hide-and-seek fashion, and lipsticks and eyebrow pencils can be considered writing instruments, perhaps mightier than either pen or sword. In other words, if "pandering to the widespread weakness for titillation" is what got Mr. Ginzburg his jail sentence, he ought to have lots of pleasant company in his cell. And it isn't I, but the decision of the U.S. Supreme Court, that is responsible for this logical *extensio ad absurdum*.

And what about the male of the species? Drab since the age of the knights, they have become a bit more colorful only recently, with the advent of the beats & hippies and their apparels & appurtenances. And male make-up has come into use again also—not the artificial kind, cool it, man, but the natural kind of make-up—the beard.

Big middle-aged spreads of printer's ink have appeared to decry the hairiness and unwashedness and general sloppiness of many of those "kids"; and the new hair-styles prevalent on campuses, it's true, often look weird, and only a blind man who also lacks the sense of smell can deny a certain pungent essence & existence surrounding them. But what—apart from the anti-Establishment protest symbolism of this natural artifice, and apart from the convenient *Weltanschauung* inherent in the refusal to fight the daily battle against decay—has not been sufficiently understood, it seems to me, is the erotic function of all this, the messages conveyed to the opposite sex, or to the same, as the case may be.

That flawed beauty is likely to be more sexy than perfect beauty is well enough known. The effect of Richard Burton's pockmarks on women, and the, thereupon, flaunting of skin lesions by young men, has also been noticed and comprehended. But the frequent strange-looking combinations of clean girl & dirty boy, or vice versa, necking on the library steps, and the said pungent essences in their wake, seem to puzzle their elders no end. Yet I have a clue for those who hold their noses while they turn them up on the college population during their campus walks. The clue is contained in one of the archetypal products of what Hollywood is dishing out to the respectable burghers day-in & night-out with unbelievable monotony. Instead of curling up, period, the kitschdiggers and miniminds with the upturned noses curl up with that bestselling trash and yet never get the message from its medium—from, for example, Harold Robbins's *The Carpetbaggers*. The revealing passage reads:

> *I sipped at the drink as she came over to me. "You don't have to take a bath on my account," she said. "That smell is kind of exciting."*
>
> *I put the drink down and walked into the bathroom, taking off my shirt. When I turned to close the door, she was right behind me. "Don't get into the tub yet," she said. "It's a shame to waste all that musky maleness."*
>
> *She put her arms around my neck and pressed her body against me. I sought her lips but she turned her face away and buried it in my shoulder. I felt her take a deep, shuddering breath. She moaned softly and the heat came out of her body like steam from an oven.*
>
> *I turned her face up to me with my hand. Her eyes were almost closed. She moaned again, her body writhing. I tugged at my belt and my trousers fell to the floor. I kicked them aside and backed her toward the vanity table along the wall. Her eyes were still closed as she leaped up on me like a monkey climbing a coconut tree.*
>
> *"Breathe slow, baby," I said as she began to scream in a tortured half whisper. "I may not smell as good as this for years."*

That kind of thing can of course do incalculable harm to the impressionable young minds of the deodorant industry. How are the hucksters going to deal with such a challenge? I own a clipping—one of my favorites—that reads, *For People Who Need a STRONGER Deodorant. Give it to Someone You Like.*

VI

Being, then, an aye-sayer to highbrow & lowbrow pornography, I am a nay-sayer to the middlebrow variety. I consider under-the-counter hard-core pornography necessary in a civilization that affirms, and lives by, the adage that variety is the spice of life but fights, via tribal morality laws and mythical "community standards," against the proposition that variety may be the spice of sexlife as well. Shuddering at the notion that any human being could continue relishing his favorite meal if it were served to him daily year-in & year-out for the rest of his life, our society yet undertakes to adapt man's natural sexual appetites to the unnatural monotonous diet of monogamy. And has the hypocrisy of simultaneously pitying those who have only taken the vow of celibacy! It comes down to the same thing anyway, in theory at least, for monogamy is based on the precept, "If two people can't have any fun (or any longer any fun) with each other, neither of them must have any fun on his own." A cruel & inhuman life sentence, if you think about it.* (There are some species of birds that are reputed to be monogamous, which makes irresistible a comment on who monogamy is for.)

As for hard-core pornography, I would quarrel with Gore Vidal who, in his above-mentioned essay in the *New York Review of Books* (fine as it otherwise was), defended pornography against the charge that it is not literature because it is apt to substitute faceless protagonists, or in fact their sex organs, for real characters.† "Yet by abstracting character," Vidal says, "and by keeping his creatures faceless and vague, the pornographer does force the reader to draw upon personal experience in order to fill in the details, thereby achieving one of the ends of all literary art, that of making the reader collaborator." The devotees of pornography comprise every stratum of society and all types of people, from the primitive to the highly sophisticated, from the decadent to the exuberantly and joyfully healthy, from sexual activists to the neurotically suppressed, and it would be quite unrealistic to generalize about them. But one of the genre's benefactions is no doubt that it provides vicarious experiences and pleasures to the timid and deprived, and they, at any rate, would find it difficult or impossible to fill in any details from their own practice; but beyond that, Mr. Vidal's claim

* The German language conveys the thought in one succinct word, *Ehekrüppel*—marriage-cripple.
† Susan Sontag ably disputes that claim in an essay in *Partisan Review*. [See pp. 131–169. Ed.]

is specious in its intimation that the best of our writers, those who can, and do, create real characters, fail to solicit thereby the reader's participation, to make him a collaborator. The good writer creates character by a cunning combination of the said and the unsaid, just as a good dress designer combines veiled intimations with outright disclosure, allowing the beholder to dress & undress on his own.

Concerning soft-core pornography, the bestselling variety that is occasionally censured but never censored and is typified by its grand old man, Mickey Spillane: its stick-in-trade is sadism, but only the socially acceptable kind that springs from hate, not lust. Sadism of any kind happens not to be my cup of absinthe, but I do prefer *Story of O* to *Kiss Me Deadly,* and not for literary reasons alone. I find cruelty in the guise of moral indignation (actually a boyscout fear & hatred of women) repulsive, and sadism disguised as patriotism, or masculine virtue (actually impotence), or just plain anger and deepseated, confused, displaced fury decidedly unattractive. All Mickey & his ilk ever put into a woman's belly is bullets—their penis surrogate; and then the hero walks proudly away, his smoking, uncocked revolver limp. The official censors find this to their liking; it represents their own mentality, for they are neither against the vicious nor the viscous, just against "vice." And violence, judging by the success of soft-core sadism offered in supermarket paperbacks, on commercial TV, and by the Hollywood industry, is closer to virtue than vice.

The Establishment and many good citizens are frightened now by the violence erupting in the ghettos. But how can they honestly and in perfect sanctimony condemn it, after they have been practicing it, in war and in peace, for so long, and enjoying it, full of popcorn bliss, enacted on silver screens? What they really deplore is not violence, but that it may be directed against *them.*

I feel only distaste for the use of sex as a weapon, rape as an instrument of revenge. "Dishonoring" a woman through sexual assault is a time-honored concept, but the sex act as a form of violence motivated by hatred and employed as a strategy in the white-power vs. black-power struggle is a new development, both in our life and our literature. Compared to this mutation, Sodom & Gomorrah were good clean fun. To me, the only acceptable view and practice of sex is the hedonistic one, and the divorce of mutual pleasure from sex the only perversion.

1 The hypocrisy may even result in rendering aid to the absurd contention that, as far as the charge of pornography is concerned, a work of art need not, and indeed should not, be judged in its entirety. Circuit Judge Manton, in the celebrated case of *United States v. One Book Entitled* Ulysses, argued that point quite cogently in his dissenting opinion: ". . . nor can the case be taken to mean that the book is to be judged as a whole. If anything, the case clearly recognizes that the book may be obscene because portions thereof are so, *for pains are taken to justify and show not to be obscene portions to which objection is made."* (My italics.) This is difficult to gainsay: the defense lawyers laid themselves wide open to that charge. Judge Woolsey, who freed Joyce's masterpiece, knew better than to take their tack. Establishing, also legally, the fact that any genuine artistic creation is bigger than the sum of its parts, his classic decision culminates in the phrase, "In respect to the recurrent emergence of the theme of sex in the minds of his characters, it must always be remembered that his locale was Celtic and his season Spring": the book's intermittent salaciousness is frankly admitted and justified as being integral to its theme—the only tenable position. Judge Woolsey's phrase, though widely familiar and reprinted in every edition of *Ulysses,* is all too often considered a mere piece of frivolous poetry and it seems worth the risk of sounding repetitious to point out its real legalistic significance.

2 There is a remarkable paucity of sexual taboo words in the English language in the first place, with most of them having to do *double entendre* duty as common household words on the one hand, and as sexually connotative terms on the other, acquiring their sexuality only in context and as secondary characteristics. Examples abound—from the Biblical euphemism "to know" to "eat," "blow," "suck," "screw," "cock," "prick," "balls," "meat," "pussy," "snatch," "gash," etc. Sometimes the case is orthographically, if not phonetically, confounded, as in "ass" which is rarely spelled "arse" and takes on an erudite and literary, not to say refined, quality in its correct (all too correct) version. The accretion of earthiness through illiteracy is manifested also in "jerk" for "jack," with the sexual connotation being supplied only by "off" in either case; that is, if one can trust the Wentworth-Flexner etymology in their *Dictionary of American Slang* which derives "jack off" from "ejaculate" and thus gives it priority over "jerk off"—which is, however, kinetically suggestive enough in itself and adds the mildly contemptuous connotation of "jerk" to the action.

Similarly, only the combination of the harmless "hard" with the harmless word "on" produces a potentially explosive taboo, while its synonym "erection" is clinical and has to do double duty again: every tourists' handbook is full of picturesque erections. So, if one considers words like "shit" and "piss" and "fart" common, but so commonly common that they're already unobscene, only "cunt" and "fuck" appear to be left as honest-to-badness dirty words, the second one at least in its primary meaning; and even though there are combinations like "motherfucker" (which has lost its literal meaning altogether and has become a racially and politically loaded invective) and "cocksucker" (also degenerated to a stronger equivalent of "bastard" or "bitch"), there is really little left to brag about in the way of a filthy vocabulary in English, as compared to, say, Hungarian—or so I hear. State legislatures and leagues of decency, bless 'em, still throw fits when they encounter these words in student newspapers and they still can't be uttered on the air, but some of our *literati* this side of the generation gap seem hellbent on extinguishing also the last remnants of the near-extinct species. For example, I read in a little magazine of not too long ago that the poet Gregory Corso, disregarding the vast entertainment differences between fucking and having sexual intercourse, proposed to eliminate that difference at least verbally by making the word "fuck" generally acceptable, which means, socially respectable. That last was not the stated intent of the campaign which he claimed was urgently needed, but it surely would be its result. Maybe he'll get a Ford Foundation grant for the project, which wouldn't surprise me too much in view of some other foundation-supported endeavors one hears about. However, since we're so close to Mr. Corso's goal already, no official aid may be needed.

William Phillips

Writing About Sex

SINCE SEX IS OLDER THAN LITERATURE, ONE WOULD THINK IT IS entitled to more respect. But the relation has always been just the reverse; literature has always been protected against the encroachments of sex. Even now, when it would seem that almost anything goes, a number of serious critics have been alarmed by the lack of sexual restraint in literature, which they regard as a symptom of moral decline. Most of their fire is directed at figures like Genet, Burroughs, and Mailer, though they are generally upset by the moral tone of contemporary writing as a whole.

Now we need hardly be reminded that what goes by the name of the moral question is an old and recurrent one, popping up with almost every new generation, as new sensibilities and new attitudes about the limits of literature come up against old ones. Today the split is wider, though the old values are frequently being defended by more sophisticated people, who themselves were brought up on the idea that art made its own rules. This means only that the confusion is on a higher level. The new values, on the other hand, are supported by people who make a principle of going out of bounds in every possible way—in morals, in sex, in art. Much of the new writing represents not so much a break with an existing tradition as with the very idea of tradition, while those who are holding the line against the so-called new barbarians claim they are defending not some philistine standards but literature itself, and some even go so far as to insist they are protecting the very basis of civilization. Those who feel themselves responsible for the health of art and society have been warning us that what we have is a free-for-all and not the normal kind of experiment and innovation prescribed for progress in the arts.

As things shape up, there seems to be some conflict between the idea of freedom and the idea of civilization—which is nothing new to those who know their Freud and have followed the diversions of Norman O. Brown and his less theoretical cothinkers. Until recently, however, anyone claiming to be advanced had to be for both freedom *and* civilization, though naturally the emphasis varied and there was usually a good deal of vagueness when it came to defining just what one meant and how it applied to art. Now things have changed: freedom literally means going all the way, turning everything on; but civilization today is actually regarded with a certain amount of irony and skepticism, particularly by those who have an adventurous attitude to life and to art, and, of course, by those who think of civilization as a synonym for a corrupt and dying system.

This, I think, is roughly the way the lines are drawn at present. In literature sex is often the issue, though other moral questions are involved. But when we try to examine more exactly what people are for and where certain works stand the picture is not so clear. In some contemporary writing commercial motives have gotten mixed up with what might have been a normal extension of the frontiers of sex and morality. Also different kinds of sex and different uses of them for literary or ideological—or commercial— purposes are not always distinct and they tend to be lumped together under the heading of the new. On the other side of the fence, the guardians of civilized art are hard to pin down, once we get beyond the generalities on which most of us are bound to agree. Often, you can't tell whether they are objecting to violations of current morality, or of current taste, whether there is too much sex, or it is too detailed or too eccentric—in short, whether the objections are literary, or moral, or ideological or just squeamish.

Usually the case against the new sexuality is not made too explicit. But two recent pieces by George P. Elliott (*Harper's,* March, 1965) and George Steiner (*Encounter,* October, 1965) * do take fairly clear stands. Both Elliott and Steiner claim to be talking mainly about pornography, though they are really talking about sex and its moral and aesthetic limits in literature, and about moral values in general. At bottom, Elliott's position is that too much sex is bad not only for literature but for society. At first he argues that to keep a safe distance from sex, as from other bodily functions, is simply a matter of good taste, though his argument would seem to have more to do with psychology than with aesthetics.

> *We have a certain sense of specialness about these voluntary bodily functions each must perform for himself— bathing, eating, defecating, urinating, copulating, performing the sexual perversions from heavy petting to necrophilia. Take eating, for example. There are few strong taboos around the act of eating; yet most people feel uneasy about being the only one at the table who is, or who is not, eating, and there is an absolute difference between eating a*

* These two essays appear on pp. 72–95 and 96–108 respectively.

*rare steak washed down by plenty of red wine and watch-
ing a close-up of a movie of someone doing so. One wishes
to draw back when one is actually or imaginatively too
close to the mouth of a man enjoying his dinner; in exactly
the same way one wishes to remove oneself from the presence of a man and woman enjoying sexual intercourse. Not
to withdraw is to peep, to pervert looking so that it becomes a sexual end in itself. As for a close-up of a private
act which is also revolting, a man's vomiting, say, the avoidance-principle is the same as for a close-up of steak-eating,
except that the additional unpleasantness makes one wish
to keep an even greater distance.*

But then he proceeds to connect excessive sexuality with
politics and with morality. All the pillars of our existence,
according to Elliott—the family, government, society, and
civilization itself—all are threatened when sex is on the
loose. "Indecency," he says, "is put to politically dangerous
uses." Furthermore, he says, if one is for civilization, "for
even our warped but still possible society in preference to
the anarchy that threatens from one side or the other," then
one has to sacrifice "some sensuality of the irresponsible."
This irresponsible sensuality, Elliott explains, is mostly to
be found in "the politically repressed." "This would help to
account," he goes on, "for the apparently greater sensuality
among American Negroes than among American whites.
. . ."

What all this sexual and political irresponsibility adds up
to for Elliott is the dread disease of nihilism, which by his
definition "would dissolve both the state and the family in
the name of unrestricted gratification of natural appetite."
The principal carriers are Genet, Burroughs, and Henry
Miller, though other writers, like Baldwin, are slightly in-
fected. For some reason, however, the most subversive is
Miller, whose sexual deviations and social estrangement Elliott regards as a menace to literature and society.

*Again and again he represents the sexual antics of his char-
acters as evidence of desperation, lurking behind the total*

despair of meaninglessness. He is what he says he is: an enemy not just of the badness of our society, not just of our specific society, but of society as such. To do what he can to get his readers also to become enemies of society, he assaults with persuasive force taboos, especially sexual taboos, which are intrinsic to the social order. . . . As an act against society, to write, publish, and distribute a book like Tropic of Cancer *is more serious than to write, publish, and distribute a pamphlet which intellectually advocated the forcible overthrow of the government, but less serious than to take arms against the government—about on a par with inciting to rebellion. . . . In other words, the only plausible argument for suppressing* Tropic of Cancer *would be that its publication is a dangerous political act and not that the book is pornographic, even though its pornography is the main instrument of the book's nihilistic force.*

Steiner's argument is more sophisticated. He, too, is disturbed by the lack of inhibition in pornography or in any other kind of writing. But his objection to too much sexual exposure is essentially that it makes public something that should remain private and restricts the imagination because sex has a limited repertoire. "Sexual relations are, or should be," says Steiner, "one of the citadels of privacy, the night-place where we must be allowed to gather the splintered, harried elements of our consciousness to some kind of inviolate order and repose." This sexual homily has little to do with writing for it is really an argument against acts of exhibitionism or voyeurism, though its view of sex as reassuringly serene and relaxing—almost as good as a warm bath—and free of mystery or terror has literary implications. Steiner's seemingly more effective point is that there are only a limited number of sexual variations; hence, for Steiner, the vague and less erotic descriptions of sexual activity, of the kind one finds in writers like Stendhal, George Eliot, Tolstoy, or Henry James, are more suggestive, hence more imaginative, than exact or charged descriptions of sexual relations could be. This, it seems to me, is not true, and, anyway, the comparison is unhistorical; but it is at least an arguable position. Like Elliott, however, Steiner introduces moral and political considerations when he claims that "the novels being produced under the new code of total statement . . . leave man less free, less himself, than they found him. . . ." In other words, it is nothing short of human freedom that is at stake when fiction loses its earlier reserve in handling sex and goes in for erotic detail.

There is simply no evidence to indicate that sex is robbed of its power and mystery and the range of feeling or thinking is narrowed when sex is treated as freely as any other kind of experience. On the contrary writers like D. H. Lawrence, Nabokov, or Mailer cannot be said to have narrowed our views of sex or interfered with our freedom. It seems to me that Steiner does not like certain kinds of writing, which is his critical right, but what he is really doing is elevating his taste into an intellectual principle.

As for Elliott, I need scarcely point out that his social views are as conservative as his idea of literature. If there is a lesson to be drawn, it is that the two often go together; though recently some political radicals have turned out to be quite conservative in their literary tastes. It is impossible ever to prove such things, but I suspect that one cannot rule out *some* new things without invoking a principle that would rule out *any* new things. If certain kinds of writing or thinking are to be excluded, either because they are immoral or bad for art, it can be done only in the name of some existing norms or values, which are assumed to be fixed, and, therefore, outside of time and history. How else can one justify, for example, saying that Miller's or Genet's or Mailer's treatment of sex is out of bounds, except by appealing to notions of sex and morality of the most conventional kind.

Are we then to conclude that we cannot legitimately set any limits for sexuality—or for anything else—in literature? If by limits we mean arbitrary, *a priori* principles, rules of restraint, it would seem that we cannot impose any such limits without getting into some kind of intellectual if

not legal censorship. Even if the taboos are advanced in the
name of literature itself, they are in effect an attempt to outlaw a less restricted sensibility.

It might be objected that if no limits can be put on literature, then the role of criticism becomes limited. If anything
goes, then there is no basis for literary or intellectual values.
However, I am not proposing the abdication of criticism;
what I have been suggesting is simply that restraint is an indirect form of criticism, and a very conservative one. Some
critics might dismiss such an approach as extraliterary, but
in the sense that every judgment, like every new work, is a
stand in favor of certain kinds of art and against others—
in this sense the literary moralists, in their objections to uninhibited writing, are asserting their preference for another
kind of literature. Thus Elliott's remarks about sex and society might be said to be a critical statement, though a fairly
conventional one, for his disgust with oversexed writing is
actually an endorsement of undersexed, respectable, responsible, unalienated writing that is not too critical of existing
society. Similarly, Steiner's distaste for sexual abandon or detail is connected with a nostalgia for the classics. In fact,
most moralizing critics rarely propose genuine literary alternatives in the present; hence they are usually scolding contemporary writers in the name of some nonexistent moral or
literary purity and responsibility that presumably existed in
the past. But this moral Utopia, this myth of propriety and
good taste, however vague, arbitrary, and illusory, is the ideological equivalent of writing that is not so far out or has already been assimilated.

Editors of popular magazines know very well the distinction between old and new sensibilities, though they find it
profitable to treat them as fashions. They are able to trade
on the appetite for the new, which is increased by the moral
resistance to it, by feeding respectable audiences more and
more outrageous writing, so that things that used to be beyond the pale now have become old hat. Of course, this is
due partly to a natural loosening up in matters of sex and

morals, but it is also because the forbidden has been artificially inseminated into writing. The result is a kind of manufactured chaos, that is numbing the capacity of frivolous
people to be shocked, and making it more and more difficult
for serious people to think clearly about what is going on.
Some writers and critics (like Fiedler) have been rushing to
sign up for the future, while others (like Elliott) are busy
frantically shoring up the past.

One result of the attempt to merchandize the new sexuality is the confusion between literature and pornography. (I
should say I do not believe in any bans on pornography, but
if there is a problem, it is legal and social, not literary.)

It has been argued by Susan Sontag * that pornography on a
certain level, like *Story of O* (and possibly even *Fanny Hill*)
is a form of literature. Her argument, which is quite powerful and original, is that the pornographic imagination presents a total vision of sex and experience not unlike other
extreme kinds of writing, and that it is not just a recital of
sexual acts for purposes of excitation. Still, I think this view
might not be incompatible with the idea that there can be
good and bad pornography; for I am not sure it completely
breaks down the distinction between the genre of pornography and literature.

One aspect of pornography, however, does seem pertinent
to the question of sexuality in contemporary fiction, and suggests a link between pornography and literature. The standard form of pornography is usually perverse † and violent in
a way that suggests some need to overthrow or transform accepted ideas of the sexual relation. Usually the hero is a victimized woman—or, more frequently, a girl—who is
used and abused—rarely used up—and the plot is the
story of all the things a man could imagine perpetrating on
her. Yet the narrative, which is a male fantasy, is usually told
ostensibly from the innocent point of view of the woman

---

* See pp. 131–169.
† I am using the term perverse in its conventional sense, though, obviously
the concept of perversity needs re-examination.

who has been violated, as though the author is acting out his fantasies both as a man and as a woman. The obvious example is *Fanny Hill*. And though *Story of O* has been rumored to have been written by a woman, it seems to be the same kind of male fantasy—which might suggest the beginning of a pornographic convention.

One can only guess at the meaning of this kind of sexual conversion. But what is particularly interesting is that a similar kind of converted, mechanized, and dispersed sexuality is found in modern writing that cannot be dismissed as pornography. We see it in Burroughs, in Genet; and there is a good deal of perversity and ambiguity in Mailer's willful sexuality (as there was in D. H. Lawrence); in Selby's sadism; in Henry Miller's acting out of boyish dreams; in Pynchon's bizarre connections; in John Barth's pan-sexuality, which by making everything possible normal, creates a system of comic perversity.

There is clearly a new kind of sexuality in modern fiction: not just more sex, but a different kind of sex, one that is undoubtedly related to the new moods and the new styles of living today. In the past, even in unconventional writers like Joyce or Lawrence or Kafka, the treatment of sex usually was quite straightforward and not very far from the conventions of sex, even though there were occasional perverse implications. The most daring of the earlier novels rarely strayed beyond the heterosexual mold; when they went in for sexual detail it was mostly to describe intense passion or extramarital escapades. One might say they sublimated the more erotic and perverse drives into ambiguities of motive and feeling. Henry James is, of course, a classic instance. An example of how far the traditional novelist permitted himself to go is the story told in Stavrogin's confession in *The Possessed*. But this is an isolated episode, and the psychological underground revealed in it is dispersed in Stavrogin's character and politics, as it probably is in many other of Dostoevsky's obsessive figures and situations.

Of all the writers who have gone in for perversity, Mailer is probably the least perverse. Though his last novel, *An*

American Dream, has come in for a good deal of scolding, it seems to me most of the critics have been shocked by only two things, the unconventional sexuality and the attitude toward the murder. If we ask what actually goes on sexually in the novel that might be considered off limits, I suppose the one thing that stands out is the anal preoccupation. But it is hard to see on what ground this fixation—which Swift and Lawrence also had—could be banned in literature, any more than any other obsessive idea. What is more questionable is the liberating force with which it is endowed by Mailer, as it apparently was, too, by Lawrence, though less explicitly. It is thus the sexual philosophy and not the fantasy or the act that one might be critical of in literary terms. As for other sexual eccentricities in *An American Dream,* the only ones worth noting are the sharing of women in a semi-incestuous way—as Rojack does with his father-in-law—and the heightened sexuality after the murder. But these, too, are obviously matters for literary—or psychological—analysis, not for approval or disapproval.

Some established critics have also charged Mailer with immorality on the grounds that Rojack is neither punished enough nor made to feel guilty enough for the murder of his wife. Now, aside from the primitive notion of the morality of modern literature inherent in such an accusation, whose source is to be found in popular culture, it represents a misreading of the novel. Mailer's novel is obviously a fantasy in which certain sexual obsessions are merged with visions of omnipotence and with fits of frustration. This is not an uncommon fantasy, even though it borders on the psychotic in its utter self-indulgence; but somewhere at the center is the little boy's fear—quite normal—that he might not make it. This fear, one might say, ties the novel to the more acceptable versions of our common experience. If one can talk of the subject of *An American Dream,* it might be said to be a fantasy of abnormal desire grounded by normal fear.

Like Mailer, Henry Miller has had to contend with literary and moral conventions. Yet, despite Miller's wild reputa-

tion, his perversity seems to be integrated into a fairly ortho-
dox brand of bohemianism. One notes again and again in
works like *Sexus* and *Tropic of Cancer* how Miller slides
from sex into observations about literature, or society or existence in general. The elusiveness of sex is entangled in the
religion of art. Somehow the footlooseness and the alienation
of the young writer is associated with an avant-garde casual-
ness and freedom in bouncing from one woman to another.
The perversity, however, is almost always just below the surface, expressing itself in such things as the failure to connect
with women, the lack of genuine pleasure, the intimation of
voyeurism and exhibitionism in sexual relations involving
groups of people and the insatiable appetite for whores,
whom Miller is always trying to convert to women in his
mind and to machines in bed. If one is to make any kind of
judgment, though, it is not that Henry Miller's sexual hap-
penings strain our capacity for novelty. On the contrary, his
prowlings and frustrations seem almost commonplace and
they succeed only in giving Miller the air of a middle-aged
schoolboy. Far from being shocking, Miller's sexual bohemianism appears dated today.

To assimilate Norman Mailer or Henry Miller one simply
has to face oneself. To assimilate writers like Genet and Burroughs one might have to redefine one's relation to an alien
experience or to an alien idea of experience as well as to
oneself. For Genet's hero, in his fiction, is a portrait of the
underground man as a homosexual and a criminal; while
Burroughs has created a homosexual spaceman who lives in
a permanent nightmare of fornication, hallucination and destruction.

Of the two, I think Genet is a much more impressive
figure than Burroughs. In my opinion, Genet's plays—
particularly *The Balcony* and *The Blacks*—are among
the outstanding works of our time. In both plays the morbid
sexuality is transformed by a bizarre and perverse system of
associations into a sense of wild being, free of moral attitu-

dinizing or social pretense. The novels, however, are narrower: here the perversity exists in its natural habitat and one cannot help see it and judge it in relation to some other system that is not so perverse. I do not mean to take down the novels: on the contrary, I think they are in their own way marvelously conceived and executed; but they are a special genre, probably a limited one, a kind of autobiography of the imagination, though of course Genet appears to be describing real events in his life.

One of the difficulties in relating to the new sexual style is the assumption that the traditional handling of sex in literature is natural and pure and that what we have today is a distortion. The fact is that there is no basic sex—in the way there might be a basic English—except biologically or clinically. Sex in literature has always been ideological: it has always been conceived of in terms of values and attitudes toward other kinds of experience. In this respect, the depiction of sex has been an enactment of an idea of sex. Thus sex has been bawdy, comic, adventurous, immoral, fulfilling, frustrating, mysterious, tragic, open, liberating. In its literary evolution sexuality has reflected various pagan, courtly, pastoral, middle-class, and romantic conventions. On the whole, though, the traditional idea of sex has been associated with individual fate, that is, with human realization or destruction, through love and passion. And it is with this sexual tradition that both pornography and the new sexuality might be said to have broken, substituting for it a deflated, polymorphous idea of sex divorced from love and from the institutionalized relations in which sex had in the past been located. It is an idea of sex that is experimental, unfettered, anarchic; and if, like more traditional views of sex, it is also represented as the expression of true being, it is based on a conception of being entirely fluid and unpredictable, and limited only by one's imagination.

The question, then, of how much perversity can be assimilated into literature has to do with the idea of sex rather than with its reality. If we can talk at all about the "reality" of sex, it would seem that a sense of its willfullness and its inventiveness, partly as an escape from its terrors, is more suggestive of the actual experience than a tasteful and restrained representation. As for one's imagination, it is even less restricted in its pursuit of erotic fantasies. Obviously, normality can no longer be regarded as a meaningful idea for writing, though it would seem that traditional values cannot be entirely disregarded. Frank Kermode recently argued that a commitment to the new, such as Harold Rosenberg advocates, means giving up all critical values, for if novelty creates its own value then the traditional method of judging new works by existing standards can no longer be applied. Kermode, it seems to me, was right in pointing to the danger of a principle that softens us up for any innovation or break with tradition. On the other hand, we run the opposite risk of opposing new styles in the name of old ones, and justifying this by failing to recognize that every new work alters old standards. It is clearly this reciprocal relation that makes for a proper balance of the new and the old, though, admittedly, it is not always easy to keep in mind that one is changing one's tastes in the act of applying them.

In practice, the less eccentric forms of the new sensibility and those which are related if only symbolically to more accepted intellectual conventions are more readily assimilated. John Barth, for example, is a less extreme figure, since sexual and social chaos are represented in his novels as metaphors for each other; as is Pynchon, in whom sexual fluidity appears to be a part of the fluidity of experience; or Susan Sontag, who in most of her writing shows herself to be more an advocate than an exponent of freewheeling sexuality. Actually, it is the more extreme figures, like Burroughs and Genet (in his novels) who pose the problem and force its definition. And though extremism is one of the means by which literature deals with typical experience, extremist writing has been successful usually when its special vision has been able to generalize the extreme of human behavior. Kafka is perhaps the outstanding example of the invention of a new style of observation by a grotesque—almost psychotic—imagination, that has become a natural style. But I am not at all sure whether it can be said of Burroughs and Genet in his fiction, and particularly of their disciples, that they have succeeded in imposing their style on our experience. Undoubtedly some of the perversity of modern writing has expressed itself in sexual cultism, especially in the less gifted writers, for whom violence, sadism and homosexuality make up a self-inclosed world, sealed off even from other forms of extreme behavior. To some extent, it is a matter of literary quality, as obviously writers like Selby or Rechy exhibit the faults of the genre more than do the larger talents. But this brings us right back to the original problem, for what is lacking in the less talented works is precisely the ability to transcend or to generalize one's sexual obsessions.

In the long run, however, the literary value of this kind of extremism is an historical rather than a theoretical question. One who thinks of himself as a participant in the contemporary scene might even contend that in raising these questions and posing them in this way, one is simply outside the intellectual moods that go into the advanced forms of contemporary writing. Undoubtedly the new sensibility reflects the current emphasis on personal freedom as a way of dissociating from the political establishment. And what is commonly regarded as perversity might be thought of as a symbol of this detachment, as it was, almost explicity, for example, in Norman O. Brown's *Life Against Death*. To be sure, sexual freedom has gone so far that one wonders what would be out of bounds if the new life style were to take over.

But if one might speculate about the future, perhaps the ideal solution would be to dissociate sex completely from morality and from politics. Who knows whether this will ever happen? But if there were no restrictions on sex, in life or literature, if sexual freedom were not thought of as a paradise for radicals and purgatory for conservatives—if sex were simply taken for granted like other neutral activities, like, say, eating or swimming, then possibly the air might be cleared so that the question of sex in literature could become a purely literary question, not a battlefield for moral and social issues. If sex were free it would have nothing to do with the idea of freedom.

Notes on the Contributors

DOUGLAS A. HUGHES is an assistant professor of English at Washington State University and the editor of three other books published in 1970: *The Way It Is, Studies in Short Fiction,* and *From a Black Perspective.*

ALBERTO MORAVIA is one of the best known contemporary Italian novelists. His most recent novel, *Command, and I Will Obey You,* was published in 1969 by Farrar, Straus & Giroux.

ANTHONY BURGESS is a prolific English writer of fiction (*Enderby,* 1968) and literary criticism (*Urgent Copy,* 1969) who now makes his home in Malta.

HARRY LEVIN is the chairman of the comparative litera-ture department at Harvard University and the author of several important literary studies, including *James Joyce, The Power of Blackness,* and *Contexts of Criticism.*

VIVIAN MERCIER was born and reared in Ireland and re-ceived his Ph.D. degree from Trinity College, Dublin. A professor of English at the University of Colorado, he is the author of *The Irish Comic Tradition* and *A Reader's Guide to the French New Novel.*

STANLEY EDGAR HYMAN, born in Brooklyn in 1919, teaches literature at Bennington College. He is the author of *The Armed Vision,* an outstanding study of modern literary criticism.

PAUL GOODMAN, educator, literary critic, and admirable social gadfly, was born in New York City in 1911. His many widely read books include *Growing Up Absurd, Compulsory Mis-Education,* and *Like a Conquered Province: The Moral Ambiguity of America.*

PETER MICHELSON is an English professor at the Uni-versity of Notre Dame and a frequent contributor to periodi-cals and quarterlies.

GEORGE P. ELLIOTT, a novelist and essayist, teaches English at Syracuse University.

GEORGE STEINER, who was born in Paris in 1929, is Fel-low and Director of English Studies at Churchill College, Cambridge University. He is the author of *Tolstoy or Dos-toevsky, The Death of Tragedy,* and *Language and Silence.*

KENNETH TYNAN was a provocative and intelligent drama critic in London before serving for several years as the literary manager of the British National Theatre. He was the deviser and organizer in 1969 of the erotic entertain-ment *Oh! Calcutta!*

ERNEST VAN DEN HAAG was born in the Nether-lands in 1914. He is now a practicing psychoanalyst and a pro-fessor of social philosophy at New York University.

SUSAN SONTAG is one of the most engaging and brilliant literary and cultural critics in America today. In addition to two books of essays, *Styles of Radical Will* and *Against Interpretation,* she has written two novels.

FELIX POLLAK was born in Austria and received a doctor of jurisprudence degree from the University of Vienna. The curator of rare books at the University of Wisconsin Library, Mr. Pollak has published two books of poetry and he writes frequently for quarterly journals.

WILLIAM PHILLIPS is the distinguished editor of *Partisan Review.*

Index